THE
PILGRIM
ROAD

THE PILGRIM ROAD

Sermons on Christian Life

✠✠✠✠✠

B. A. GERRISH

Edited by Mary T. Stimming

Westminster John Knox Press
Louisville, Kentucky

Scripture quotations from the New Revised Standard Version of the Bible are copyright © 1989 by the Division of Christian Education of the National Council of the Churches of Christ in the U.S.A. and are used by permission. Quotations from the Revised Standard Version of the Bible are copyright 1946, 1952, © 1971 by the Division of Christian Education of the National Council of the Churches of Christ in the U.S.A. and are used by permission. Quotations marked JB are from *The Jerusalem Bible*, copyright © 1966, 1967, 1968 by Darton, Longman & Todd, Ltd., and Doubleday & Co., Inc. Used by permission of the publishers. Quotations marked NJB are from The New Jerusalem Bible, copyright © 1985 by Darton, Longman & Todd, Ltd., and Doubleday & Co., Inc. Used by permission of the publishers. Quotations marked PHILLIPS are from *The New Testament in Modern English*, revised edition, translated by J. B. Phillips. © J. B. Phillips 1958, 1960, 1972. Used by permission of Macmillan Publishing Company.

"Grace Demanding" and "One Thing Certain" are reprinted by kind permission of *Criterion*. "One Thing Certian" originally appeared under the title "What Do You Know? The One Thing Certain."

Excerpt(s) from *The Way of Life* by Lao Tzu, translated by Raymond B. Blakney. Translation copyright © 1955 by Raymond B. Blakney, renewed © 1983 by Charles Philip Blakney. Used by permission of Dutton Signet, a division of Penguin Putman Inc.

Excerpt from *Saint Joan: A Chronicle Play in Six Scenes* by George Bernard Shaw is reprinted by kind permission of The Society of Authors, on behalf of the Bernard Shaw Estate.

Excerpts from *An Inspector Calls* by J. B. Priestley are reprinted by permission of the Peters Fraser and Dunlop Group Limited on behalf of the Estate of J. B. Priestley. © The Estate of J. B. Priestley 1946.

Book design by Sharon Adams
Cover design by Night & Day Design
Cover art courtesy Tony Stone Images

First edition

Published by Westminster John Knox Press
Louisville, Kentucky

This book is printed on acid-free paper that meets the American National Standards Institute Z39.48 standard. ∞

PRINTED IN THE UNITED STATES OF AMERICA

00 01 02 03 04 05 06 07 08 09—10 9 8 7 6 5 4 3 2 1

Library of Congress Cataloging-in-Publication Data

Gerrish, B. A. (Brian Albert), 1931–
    The pilgrim road : sermons on Christian life / B. A. Gerrish ;
edited by Mary T. Stimming. — 1st ed.
        p.   cm.
    Includes bibliographical references.
    ISBN 0–664–25691–0 (alk. paper)
    1. Christian life Sermons.   2. Sermons, American.   I. Stimming.
Mary T. (Mary Theresa)   II. Title.
BV4501.2.G44   1999
252—dc21   99–38816

The Balcony . . . is the classical standpoint, and so the symbol, of the perfect spectator, for whom life and the universe are permanent objects of study and contemplation.

By the Road I mean the place where life is tensely lived, where thought has its birth in conflict and concern, where choices are made and decisions are carried out.

John A. Mackay

For Joe
Companion on the Road
            B. A. Gerrish

CONTENTS

AUTHOR'S PREFACE

I could invoke the authority of my favorite theologian,
John Calvin, for the view that the first mark of the church
is the Word of God purely preached and heard. Naturally,
I should not expect Dr. Stimming, as a Roman Catholic,
to assent to a Calvinist proposition. But as I look through
the book she has put together out of my attempts to
preach, her ability to *hear* is evident to me on every page.
She has arranged these "meditations," delivered over a
time span of more than three decades, into a convincing
pattern that really does reflect my teaching and writing as
a theologian, and I am delighted that she sees the collection as a useful, if unconventional, introduction to Christian theology. She has also shown a keen editorial eye for
language that needed modification or deletion because
tied too closely to the time in which it was first spoken. I
am deeply grateful to her.

Nearly all of these brief addresses began in a university
setting. The reader will want to keep that in mind. College audiences have been taught to hear *critically* any discourse whatsoever. They voice more questions, often
more doubts, than most, and I assume that this calls for
light rather than heat from anyone who hopes to win their
attention. But I also take it for granted that any sermon,
whatever its setting, aims at such light as may challenge
the hearers to think critically about *themselves* and to renew the commitments that give their lives meaning. Of
course, there are many reasons that may bring a person to
church. But the preacher must believe that, deep down, it
is the question King Zedekiah put in secret to the prophet
Jeremiah that is being asked, "Is there any word from the
Lord?" (Jer. 37:17).

Besides Mary Stimming, I owe a debt of thanks to
Bernard Brown, former dean of the Rockefeller Memorial

Chapel at the University of Chicago, who invited me to serve as one of his "university preachers." He knew well that I understood the pulpit to belong to the vocation of a theologian, and I am grateful to him and Carol Jean, his wife, for their friendship over the years. Finally, I have dedicated this book as a token of gratitude to another valued friend: Joseph Ledwell, who must have preached more sermons in a year than I ever preached in a decade.

EDITOR'S INTRODUCTION

During the five years I had the honor of serving as B. A. Gerrish's research assistant, only once did I witness him in a state of anxiety over a theological "presentation." In these years, he had delivered numerous lectures throughout the world in his areas of internationally recognized expertise. He was a featured speaker at prestigious academic institutions and gatherings. He had approached each impressive lectern with calm self-assurance. Hence, his uncharacteristic attack of nerves intrigued me. What new invitation had prompted such discomfort? The answer, I was stunned to discover, was an upcoming date to preach at Rockefeller Chapel. No lectern, no matter how imposing, had caused him to tremble—the pulpit did.

I

I have come to learn that the pulpit produces this effect in Brian Gerrish whenever he ascends to its heights. When pressed as to why preaching and not teaching prompts such a response, he replied, tellingly, "It is one thing to be responsible to ideas, it is another altogether to be responsible to the Word of God." This is not to say that he ever took his teaching responsibilities lightly. Generations of his students at Union Theological Seminary (New York; 1957–58), McCormick Theological Seminary (Chicago; 1958–65), the University of Chicago (1965–96), and Union Theological Seminary in Virginia (Richmond; 1996–present) will attest that this is far from the truth. Rather, his statement hints at the theology of preaching he embraces and the consequent awe it evokes from ministers of the Word.

For Gerrish, preaching is sacramental. The concept of preaching as the sacramental Word has roots in Augustine, but it was chiefly developed and championed by Luther and Calvin, two peerless Reformers. Luther and Calvin advanced a doctrine of preaching that spoke of it no longer in terms of religious and moral instruction (the dominant Roman Catholic model), but in terms of transformational efficacy. In short, in place of an essentially pedagogical theory of preaching, they endorsed a sacramental one. As sacramental Word, God's self-revelation proclaimed through public reading and preaching is a means of grace, which effects what it signifies, causes what it declares, announces and mediates a real presence of Christ.

With such an exalted view of preaching, no wonder Gerrish was unsettled while he prepared his sermon! I was wrong to assume that it was concern about how his words would reflect on him that occasioned his anxiety. No, it was consciousness of his role, an awareness of God's awesome use of the preacher, that accounted for his prepreaching demeanor. According to a sacramental Word theology of preaching, God has pledged to work through preaching. In the proclaimed Word, Christ awakens and nurtures faith, exposes and forgives sins, sanctifies and redeems the believer. The preacher is thus an instrument through whom God conveys saving grace. Only ignorance or arrogance could leave a preacher unmoved by his or her role in this process.

II

In the sermon "Remembrance of Things Present," Gerrish describes the different aims of teaching and preaching:

> A lecture is supposed to contribute to that increase of knowledge to which the University [of Chicago] is dedicated. *Crescat scientia!* ("Let knowledge increase [that human life may flourish]"). The sermon, on the other hand, is to increase our commitment to some things that we know, for the most part, already.

Theologically astute and psychologically insightful, this volume is a sensitive presentation of the cardinal themes in Christian life. Perennial themes are interpreted in ways at once faithful to tradition and relevant to contemporary believers. Gerrish does not hesitate to address difficult contemporary questions germane to these themes (such as faith and science, faith and historical research), but he does so without getting lost in a sea of critical debate.

Taken together, nearly the entire range of Christian doctrine receives notice in these sermons. To magnify their systematic quality, the sermons have been arranged according to thematic rather than chronological order. They are organized around the motif of the journey of Christian life, a life in which we are pilgrims searching for truth on the road, that is, through the lived experience of our faith commitments.

Part I, "The Journey," introduces the central themes of Christian life and, not coincidentally, the central themes of Gerrish's theology: faith ("The Face of God"), new life ("Forgiveness"), and thanksgiving ("Gratitude"). In many respects, Part I offers a synopsis of the entire volume. Part II, "Hindrances," wrestles with one of the central challenges to Christian confidence—suffering. These sermons rebut the theory of divine retribution and demand action in response to human suffering ("Truth from the Road"). They reconceive God in relation to our suffering ("Evil at the Hand of God?") and proclaim that God makes brokenness whole ("The View from Eternity").

The Christian experience of hardship is transformed through faith in Christ. In Part III, "The Lightbearer," Gerrish reflects on Christian convictions about the person and work of Christ in light of contemporary concerns. Addressing the questions raised for believers by historical research, he argues that Christ is met not in past history, but in the Word ("Many Infallible Proofs," "The Christ of Faith," "The Living Word"). In response to ecumenical concerns, he affirms that Christ is uniquely preeminent for Christians ("The Preeminence of Christ") but rejects an exclusivist understanding of this doctrine ("For and Against"). Finally, he offers an example of how faith in Christ transforms the believer ("Christ the Kingmaker").

Broadly speaking, this transformation is from sinful self-absorption to loving service of others. Part IV, "Transformation," explores the rhythms of sin, grace, forgiveness, and conscience in Christian life ("Sin," "Fitting God In," "Grace Demanding"). Part V, "Response," details the chief marks of the transformed life: responsiveness to others' needs, gratitude to God, and a new relation to God. In these sermons ("The Unquenchable Flame," "Running the Race," "Justice," and "The Proof of Friendship"), Gerrish describes the multivalent nature of Christian faith.

Although Christian faith is personal, it is never private. In its origins, its being, and its scope it is communal. Part VI, "Companions," discusses various dimensions of ecclesial Christianity. It is the gospel that is the church's most precious gift ("The Real Treasure of the Church"), which gathers believers ("The Call to Worship," "The Promise of Baptism") and makes possible an encounter with the living Christ ("Remembrance of Things Present"). Even with such encounters, Part VII, "Pilgrims," makes clear that the Christian remains homo viator, a traveler ("The Immigrants," "Strangers on Earth"). The one who is saved ("The Simple Truth," "One Thing Certain") is called to reenvision and reconfigure the world ("Dreamers of the Day").

Persons familiar with Gerrish's scholarly works will no doubt recognize themes and sources dear to his heart. He is renowned as a historical and as a systematic theologian. In particular, he is known for his work on Martin Luther, John Calvin, Friedrich Schleiermacher, Ernst Troeltsch, the relation between sixteenth- and nineteenth-century Protestant theology, and several topics in dogmatic theology, particularly the Eucharist. Admittedly, several of the individuals who figure prominently in his academic essays make rare appearances in this volume (e.g., Friedrich Schleiermacher, Ernst Troeltsch). But in his sermons as in his scholarship, he concentrates on those matters which matter to Christians: the significance of the community, the centrality of Scripture, the necessity of reliance on the Word; the prevenience of grace, the nature of faith, the demands of morality; the human experience of gratitude, limits, interconnection, and renewal. As an aid to the reader, at the conclusion of the endnotes for most sermons, there are suggestions for further readings from Gerrish's writings on related topics. Of particular interest will be Gerrish's forthcoming work, on Christian dogmatics (Westminster John Knox Press), which will provide a systematic and in-depth treatment of the themes explored in the present volume.

III

The sermons collected in this volume were preached on the campus of the University of Chicago. Nearly all were given at Rockefeller Chapel, a nondenominational Christian church which attracts every variety of believer. One was given in the Divinity School's Bond Chapel when the university chapel was under repair. One was given at Christ Church Presbyterian, Chicago. Given the nature of these texts, sources of particular interest to readers are identified in the notes; extensive references are not provided, however.

Unless otherwise noted in the text, Scripture quotations are taken from the New Revised Standard Version of the Bible, which, if specified, will be marked NRSV. The sermons were composed when the Revised Standard Version of the Bible was the preference of scholars, and it has been retained if its wording is integral to the sermon. Italicized words in biblical quotations indicate emphasis added by the author.

Scripture epigraphs for "Evil at the Hand of God?" "The View from Eternity," "Many Infallible Proofs," "The Living Word," "Christ the Kingmaker," "Sin," "Grace Demanding," "The Real Treasure of the Church," and "The Promise of Baptism" are taken from the Revised Standard Version (hereafter noted RSV). The epigraph for "The Preeminence of Christ" is from the New Jerusalem Bible (NJB). The first epigraph for "The Immigrants" is from the King James Version, the second is from J. B. Phillips, *Letters to Young Churches* (London: Geoffrey Bles,

1947). The epigraph for "Strangers on Earth" is from the King James Version. All others are from the New Revised Standard Version.

My editorial responsibilities were lightened by the outstanding work of Daniel Martin, Beena Manavalan, Roger Bailey, and Jumpol Prasitporn of Dominican University, who scanned the original typewritten sermons into computer-readable format. This work was made possible by a generous grant by Dominican University. I am sincerely appreciative of the financial and technical support.

My work was further eased by my son, Michael Nikita, who maintained two daily naps long beyond what others predicted. His sleepiness allowed me to complete my tasks while enjoying his every waking moment. As always, my husband, Louis Centorcelli, shouldered more than his fair share of responsibilities while I met deadlines and wrestled with a new computer program. I am grateful for and to the two men in my life.

Without the support and encouragement of Dawn DeVries, my friend and Brian Gerrish's wife, this project would never have been realized. I am honored that she entrusted me with the editing of what is a jointly conceived undertaking. Above all, I am thankful to Brian himself. As teacher and minister, his thoughtful faith has enlightened, challenged, comforted, and inspired many. In his introduction to *Continuing the Reformation*, he comments that Christian faith requires continual reformulation—reformulation loyal to the tradition and sensitive to present needs—and thus the church always needs theologians. The church has been blessed by his own lifelong toil in the vineyard of the Lord.

MARY STIMMING

The Journey

The Face of God

"Show your face, and we will be saved."
Psalm 80:3

Every now and then, as we find ourselves struggling to hack our way out of some dense problem of life or thought, it is a single vivid phrase that turns us in the right direction. The light goes on. The problem doesn't disappear, but in the moment of discernment we see how to come at the problem from a fresh angle. In the realm of religion, it is likely to be a striking image or metaphor, not an exact formula, that turns the switch: it captures the imagination and stirs the heart, and the intellect has to catch up later. For me, it was the image of God's "face."

I

We had been talking about a basic enough religious term: "faith." We went dutifully through the pertinent materials in the Old and New Testaments, with the help of the Bible dictionaries. Then we turned to the theologians: Thomas Aquinas (c. 1225–74), Martin Luther (1483–1546), and John Calvin (1509–64). We looked at a distinguished historian of religions, and we looked at the writings of a few psychologists and philosophers. Knowledge grew from more to more, but so perhaps did our confusion: we were a little overwhelmed by it all. For me, at least, the light went on when we were reading Calvin. (Calvin is often my inspiration, as my friends will testify—with more or less amazement and disdain.)

Calvin does not begin very promisingly. He rushes too quickly into polemic, and you know things are going to get complicated when he says we must recognize that the word "faith" is ambiguous. Ah, I thought, he sounds like one of us. What serious discussion among us doesn't begin with the recognition of ambiguity? Every question invites the unavoidable answer: "It depends on what you mean by that." Calvin does offer his own definition of "faith" and takes it apart piece by piece. But at one point—quite unexpectedly—he finds just about all he wants to say in that half a verse from Psalm 80 that I have taken as my text: "Show your face, and we will be saved."

What has that to do with faith? Well, the faith that saves us takes place when, amid the bundle of events that make up our lives, we recognize a face. And by being "saved" Calvin does not mean just being assured of a life hereafter (though he certainly doesn't leave that out). He means being safe, here and now, because all the hostility (as he puts it) is done away with once God's face is shown. We are no longer anxious, but secure: confident that, come what may, it's going to be all right. Faith does not guarantee long life, success, or affluence. But once God has shown God's face, we know that God's loving-kindness is better than life (Ps. 63:3); and though we walk through the valley of the shadow of death, we will fear no evil (Ps. 23:4).

"Show your face, and we will be saved." That is what faith—*saving* faith—is all about: whatever else we may eventually want to add, faith, to begin with, is simply recognizing the face of God. When the light went on for me, I knew I would have to preach on Calvin's text some time, and I have kept close to his version of it (which follows the old Latin Bible). Our English versions have "Cause thy face to *shine*" (KJV) or "Let your face *shine*" (NRSV). I like "show" because the psalmist is protesting the disappearance of God: God's absence or hiddenness. But I admit that our English versions are correct.

Now Calvin knew what God's face must look like: It is, he says, a *fatherly* countenance that God lifts up on us. There is, of course, nothing unusual about the paternal features of Calvin's God: "Father" has been the preferred name of God among Christians. Less usual: Calvin sometimes notes that God is also like a mother, and he seems to think that in some ways this is a better comparison. Here he differs from one of his favorite classical authors. Seneca (c. 4 B.C.E.–65C.E.) can tell you why God is like a father and not like a mother. Fathers and mothers don't show affection the same way. Father insists that the children must be called early to get on with their assignments, and he will not let them be idle even on holidays. He draws sweat from them, sometimes tears. But Mother caresses the children on her lap, keeps them out of the sun, wants them never to cry, or be unhappy, or have to work. God, Seneca concludes, loves with a manly love like Father.

Not so Calvin, who had some remarkable Scripture passages to take into account (especially Isa. 42:14; 49:15). Calvin thinks the strength of God's care fits the love of a mother too, whose devotion to her baby leaves a father's love a long way behind. In the Bible, God does not call Israel just God's "children," but God's "baby." With an almost boyish wonder, Calvin remarks: "The affection a mother feels for her baby is amazing. She fondles it in her lap, feeds it at her breast, and watches so anxiously over it that she passes sleepless nights, continually wearing herself out and forgetting about herself." What for Seneca was a weaker love, Calvin saw as stronger. Faith, then, let's say, is recognizing the fatherly or motherly face of God.

II

So far, so good. But now we need to consider a difficulty that will very likely have occurred to you as it did to me, as soon as I began thinking about my text. There seem to be two quite contradictory strands in what the Bible says about the face of God. The one strand, as we've seen, identifies salvation with seeing God's face. The other insists that to see God's face is impossible: God dwells in unapproachable light (1 Tim. 6:16).

Our psalm does reflect a sense of God's remoteness, but only as temporary absence: it pleads with God to come back and show the divine face. The psalm was written at a time when Israel was being devastated by its neighbors, who tramped in and plundered at will, laughing at Israel's

powerlessness to stop them. Was it for nothing that the
Lord had brought the chosen people out of Egypt and
planted them in a new land, driving out the old inhabi-
tants? God is asked repeatedly to show God's face. My
text from verse 3 reappears in verses 7 and 19, and it must
have appeared originally at the end of all five stanzas of the
psalm. It was no doubt the congregation's response in a
litany of complaint at the absence of God.

Similar entreaties can be found elsewhere in the Psalter
for God to "show your face" (Pss. 4:6; 31:16; 67:1;
119:135; cf. 44:3). And, of course, the familiar Aaronic
blessing contains the self-same image: "The LORD make
his face to shine upon you . . . ; the LORD lift up his countenance upon you" (Num. 6:25–26).

But then there's the other strand. When Moses asks to
see God's glory, the answer is: "You cannot see my face;
for no one shall see me and live" (Ex. 33:20). From his safe
hiding place in the rock, Moses was allowed only to catch
a glimpse of God's back as God passed by—or, as the old
King James Version has it, God's "back parts." This, too,
represents a well-established strand in Scripture, even
though some—including Moses!—are said to have met
God face to face (Ex. 32:30; 33:11; cf. Judg. 6:22; 13:22).
"No one has ever seen God" (John 1:18). God "dwells in
unapproachable light, whom no one has ever seen or can
see" (1 Tim. 6:16).

I will not try to sort out the apparent inconsistencies.
(That's not the way we are supposed to read the Bible
these days.) We are being admonished, I take it, not to
imagine that we ever have access to the divine majesty—
even when we are permitted to see that God means us
well. The divine mystery remains a mystery even in revelation. But this does pose a question for us: *How*, then,
does God show God's face? There may be a clue in the
story we read as our Old Testament lesson.

Jacob has cheated his brother Esau out of his birthright
and dreads meeting him again. Hearing that Esau is coming to meet him with four hundred men, Jacob divides his
own company and possessions into two groups, one of
which may possibly escape while Esau falls on the other
(Gen. 32:8). He prays to God for deliverance, but falls

back on some worldly diplomacy too: he sends his servants ahead in relays with extravagant gifts. To his astonishment, Esau runs to meet him, embraces him, and calls him "brother": "I have enough, my brother; keep what you have for yourself" (33:9). Not quite able to trust his ears, Jacob presses Esau to take all the gifts, and adds: "To see your face is like seeing the face of God" (v. 10).

"To see your face is like seeing the face of God"! A shrewd piece of flattery? Perhaps. But Luther, at least, was convinced that Jacob must have actually discerned the face of God in the face of his brother. I would like to think that Luther was right, since that is exactly the way God usually shows the divine face. We aren't often favored with direct theophanies, but God appears to us daily in a brother or a sister. And I don't doubt that Jacob, even as he cautiously made his deal, received a revelation of grace in the undeserved kindness of his brother. That's the way it is (mostly) with ourselves, when God chooses to show the divine face: it is through a human face.

We find ourselves trying endlessly to cover up some past fault or failure, until forgiveness assures us that grace, not guilt, must have the last word. No cover-up, no deals are needed. In someone who knows all about us and calls us "brother" or "sister" anyway, we see God's face, and we are saved.

We look out on a scene of appalling hatred, bigotry, and violence, and we are tempted to despair of the human race. Then a face appears in the crowd to remind us of justice and mercy. The pattern of events is refigured. It becomes a story of human courage and decency, which lays a task on us, enlists our support, demands that we take sides. The mysterious force that moves our lives takes on a face, and we are persuaded that justice and mercy too, like grace, are written into the constitution of our world. We see God's face, and we are saved. Saved from what? From the cynicism and despair, the resignation and indifference, that might otherwise turn us to stone.

Or perhaps we dare to look into the children's ward of a hospital and trace the last days of an eight-year-old girl with an inoperable tumor. This, as some of you will know, is what Nina Herrmann Donnelley did in a deeply moving book. She needed a theology, she says, that would get her through the questions that crowded into her mind as she watched. So do we all, even if we would rather think about something else. Though not a formal work of theology, her book does give us much of what we need. She writes of her growing respect for the nurses, whose care reflected a "Greater Love that shines through them on their patients, on each other, and on their profession." And she writes of the child's unbroken sense of security in the love of her family. In the words of our text (once again): "Show your face, and we will be saved."

III

One final word. There's no denying that God's presence is sometimes hidden from us; otherwise the prayer of the psalmist would be unnecessary. But when that happens, the fault may be our own. Recall Philip's impulsive demand: "Lord, show us the Father, and we will be satisfied" (John 14:8). He was right, of course: to see the Fatherly image really is enough. But why didn't he see it? Jesus responds with a rebuke. Has he been with his disciples for so long, and yet they still don't know him? Anyone who has seen him has seen the Father (v. 9).

In the moment of crisis, even the disciples who had lived and worked with Jesus could let their hearts be troubled. They did not cease to believe in God, but they had not learned to let Jesus be the measure of what they believed about God. This, I think, must be the meaning of those surprising words: "Believe in God; believe also in me" (14:1). If the story of Christ is the measure of what we believe, we are unlikely to expect that the presence of God in our lives will always be too plain to miss. It is a story of pain and conflict, in which the last word but one is: "Why have you forsaken me?" (Mark 15:34). Not, to be sure, the last word of all! But there is no way to get around it. "It is the God who said, 'Let light shine out of darkness,' who has shone in our hearts to give the light of the knowledge of the glory of God in the face of Jesus Christ" (2 Cor. 4:6).

Forgiveness

"Your sins are forgiven."
Luke 7:48

Recently, I was reading the prophet Micah with my family. We came to those marvelous words near the end: "Who is a God like you, pardoning iniquity . . .?/You will cast all our sins/into the depths of the sea" (Micah 7:18–19). Who is a God like you? The prophet's question carried my thoughts back to my student days, when I used to help out occasionally in an East London mission. (That was before the first Labor government had quite taken welfare out of the hands of the churches.) The superintendent and staff of the mission were all good people, beyond ordinary goodness. True, they were earthy saints, some of them, not cut for stained-glass windows. The superintendent owed his amazing success in keeping a crowd quiet to an unusual talent: the unerring accuracy with which he could aim a hymnbook at a troublemaker's head. (My own, more genteel methods escalated every minor disturbance into pandemonium.) But, without a doubt, the superintendent was a good man: he loved his people, and they loved him in return. It was the same with all the other workers.

They came to mind as I was reading Micah because there was one hymn they always sang with special energy and passion. The tune is fixed indelibly in my mind, and the refrain began with the words (sung fortissimo): "Who is a *pardoning* God like Thee?" Each time we came back to the refrain, "Who is a *pardoning* God like Thee?" I marveled that—for these devout, hardworking laborers in the Lord's vineyard—it was the forgiveness of their sins that gave them their "peak" religious experiences. I concluded that there cannot be any objective scale on which to measure guilt or gratitude: everything must depend on how seriously you take both your sins and the ever-new gift of forgiveness.

The words of the prophet are, in effect, a challenge to the gods of the heathen—not to see who's strongest, but who's the most forgiving. The New Jerusalem Bible translates: "What God can compare with you for pardoning guilt?" A little pedestrian, perhaps, but the translation brings out the prophet's challenge: Isn't the forgiving God of Israel incomparable? I shall have to leave it to the historians of religion to give the answer. It may be significant that, when I looked for an article on "pardon" or "forgiveness" in our latest *Encyclopedia of Religion*, I found none. But, of course, the possibility of a new beginning that leaves the past behind is a common religious theme. There must be a deep longing in the human heart to make a fresh start, to become a new person, to take a new name, to be born again.

For biblical faith, the new birth is forgiveness—coming to trust in a God who takes away sins (Ps. 103:12), tramples them underfoot (Micah 7:19), throws them away (Isa. 38:17), casts them (like so much nuclear waste!) into the depths of the sea (Micah 7:19), blots them out, and remembers them no more (Isa. 43:25; cf. 1:18). The story of Jesus' encounter with the woman who was a sinner is perhaps the most memorable New Testament illustration of this theme.

I

The story as we have it is found only in Luke, though it parallels in some respects the anointing at Bethany, of which we read in the other three Gospels (Mark 14:3–9; Matt. 26:6–13; John 12:1–8); and it invites comparison with the story of the woman caught in adultery in John 8. The passage in Luke 7, which we read as our Gospel lesson, has long been the subject of disagreement among interpreters. It takes the form of an anecdote containing a parable. The anecdote tells how an intruder at a dinner washed Jesus' feet and anointed them with oil, and it seems to make the woman's act of love the reason that she was forgiven her sins. "Her sins, which are many, are forgiven; for she loved much" (v. 47, KJV [the Greek is *hoti*, "because"]). But the parable says, very plainly, that both of the two debtors loved (in varying degrees) because their debts had been canceled. The only question is which will love more, for "the one to whom little is forgiven, loves little" (v. 47). So, is love the cause or the consequence of the remission of sins?

The difference is not a small one. It is hardly too much to say that it is the difference between two ways of being religious, or, at least, two ways of understanding our relationship with God; and each is likely to color everything else. Does one come before the Lord with tokens of penitence to obtain pardon, or with thankfulness because one is pardoned already? Modern scholars have argued that Luke, or someone else before him, must have put together an anecdote and a parable that just don't fit. But please let me assume for now, without argument, that St. Luke knew what he was doing and meant what he said, and that the parable really does serve to explain the anecdote, not to contradict it.

There are three characters in the story, which gets its point from the interaction between them. We call it the story of the woman who was a sinner. But it is, in fact, about three persons: the forgiven, the unforgiving, and the forgiver.

II

Consider, first, the forgiven woman. A Pharisee named Simon invites Jesus to dinner; we are not told why. The company remove their sandals, as was the custom, and recline beside the table with their feet stretched out behind them. A woman, known to the host by her dubious reputation, enters uninvited and stands behind Jesus, crying. Nobody stops her—neither Jesus nor anyone else—as she proceeds to wash his feet with her tears, then dries them

on her hair, kisses them, and rubs oil on them. An amazing, even slightly uncomfortable, display of emotion!

Who was she? All we are told directly is that she was a
known sinner, and most readers assume that she was a
town prostitute. But we can infer, at least, that she must
have known of Jesus, and very likely had met him. Otherwise, there is no reason that she should have followed him
into the house uninvited (v. 37). As Luke places the story,
it is clearly linked with the accusation—just mentioned—
that Jesus made himself a friend to sinners (v. 34). The
woman's astonishing act of love can only have been in response to the Savior's act of taking her into his friendship,
despite her sins—which is to say, his act of forgiving her.
The words of absolution, "Your sins are forgiven," important though they are, simply declare the way things already stand between them.

The psychologists tell us how crippling it can be to har-
bor guilt, and how liberating it is to throw the burden of
guilt aside. Sometimes, they blame us religious people for
sowing the guilt in the first place. But if we do, we must
have mislaid the gospel. The confession of sin can only be,
for the Christian, a confession of praise for sins forgiven.
There is a wonderful extravagance, a lack of decorum,
about the woman's devotion to her Savior. In other places,
it is true, Jesus makes obedience the proof of love (John
15:14; 21:15–19; cf. 1 John 3:14). Here, it is the sheer, un-
restrained exuberance of love that we see, and the Savior
accepts it as his due. Love goes beyond duty: it is mixed
with that profound sense of thankfulness that I witnessed
at the East London mission. Which brings me to the second character in Luke's story—the one who so plainly
lacks the love that springs from thankfulness.

III

Consider the unforgiving Pharisee. The Pharisees, I
am afraid, get a bad press in our Christian Scriptures, and
we must admit that the Gospels often give us symbolic
characters, not balanced historical portraits. The Jewish
scholar Martin Buber (1878–1965) held that Jesus was

actually closer to the best of Pharisaism than the Apostle
Paul was to Jesus. We won't argue about that now. The
question is: What do the Pharisees of the Gospels sym-
bolize? What do they stand for? The answer is: They
stand for a religion of dutifulness that likes to contrast itself with the shortcomings of anyone less devout, or virtuous, or inflexible than they are. The Pharisees of the
Gospels are not wicked people. They are, no doubt, con-
scientious family men. They are good neighbors, who
maintain property values in the neighborhood. They support their local church. All very important things! But
they are too preoccupied with other people's failures. Simon could not do as the Lord had done—put the woman's
sins behind him and let them go. He remembered them,
and they defined the woman for him: she was a sinner. If
Jesus were a real prophet, Simon thought, he would have
known what sort of woman she was (v. 39). But it was Simon, not the woman, who earned Jesus' rebuke, because
compared to her he was loveless.

Why are the censorious so censorious? That's a good
question, which has, I suspect, more answers than one. Perhaps they feel reassured of their own dutifulness if they can
concentrate on a sin they have not committed and may have
no inclination to commit. The Master's reply on another
occasion was: "Let anyone among you who is without sin
be the first to throw a stone" (John 8:7)—he didn't say anyone who hasn't committed *this* sin. The censorious among
us need to be reminded that they are given a conscience for
their personal use, to judge their own behavior and not
everyone else's. It is not the height of godliness to ask,
What does the Lord require of *them?* (Cf. Micah 6:8.) Sins
come in all shapes and sizes, which is why we need to be on
our guard against becoming crusaders against one sin only.

"You Pharisee," says Augustine, "you love little because you imagine that little is forgiven you. Not that little
really is forgiven you, but you think little of what is
forgiven you."

We are told that in a vision a saint witnessed the appearance of Satan before the judgment seat of God. Satan
protests: "I sinned only once. Why do you condemn me

and spare thousands whose sins were many?" The Lord replies: "Did you ever once ask for forgiveness?"

In one of his most sobering pronouncements, Jesus warns us that if we don't forgive, we won't be forgiven (Matt. 6:14; cf. Luke 17:3–4). I cannot believe he meant that God simply refuses to forgive the unforgiving by way of punishment. He meant, rather, that divine pardon—the word of absolution—simply can't get through to them. They lose the capacity to accept for themselves what they refuse to others. For it is surely harder to accept pardon than to give it: to be pardoned, you have to admit that you were wrong.

But we cannot doubt that Christ's mission is as much to the unforgiving as to anyone else—for those also whose religion is more a matter of grim duty than of grateful love. He accepts the invitation to eat and drink with them too, no less than with the tax collectors and notorious sinners (see also Luke 11:37; 14:1)

IV

Consider lastly, then, Christ the forgiver. It is remarkable that God is not named once in this Lukan story. But the message is clear, that in Christ God was reconciling people, not counting their trespasses against them (2 Cor. 5:19). Jesus pronounces the word of absolution, "Your sins are forgiven." And the dinner guests understand very well. "Who is this who even forgives sins?" (v. 49). He speaks with the voice of God (cf. Mark 2:7; Matt. 9:3; Luke 5:21).

In the Gospels, it is Jesus who mediates the divine pardon by eating and drinking with sinners, including those who don't realize they are sinners. That, in a word, is the meaning of Christian forgiveness: being taken into the company of the Lord, where you are accepted despite everything. And he, in turn, accepts the homage of those who live by trust, gratitude, and love, not by exact payment of their debts. Like the debtors in the parable, they have found that they cannot pay. But they believe the one who speaks the word of absolution to them: "Your sins are forgiven. . . . Your faith has saved you; go in peace" (vv. 48, 50).

Gratitude

(Convocation Sunday)

"What do you have that you did not receive?"
1 Corinthians 4:7

"What do you have that you did not receive? And if you received it, why do you boast as if it were not a gift?" A gift? That's not a text for an academic community, but for an enclave of dogmatic theologians! And just think what a lot of trouble it made for Bishop Augustine (354–430)! He finally decided that even the faith by which we receive the gifts of God must itself be a gift of God, due simply and solely to the election of grace. Otherwise, there would be one thing that is our own doing, not received by the sheer bounty of God. It must be God alone, then, who makes us differ. Thus far Augustine. And he landed in a morass of questions about divine election and human free will from which later theologians have never quite been able to extricate themselves.

Now, I have not found any more effective way to arouse a sleepy class of theology students than to mention that, according to the greatest theologians of the church, we are not masters of our destiny. True, a similar message can sometimes be heard in a literature class on the other side of the campus, or a class in the social sciences. But it is easier to be indignant with God than with our genes, our environment, or iron fate. Can it be the grace of God that finds two in the field, and takes one and leaves the other (Matt. 24:40)? Is our destiny entirely at the disposal of an arbitrary and inscrutable divine will, while our own enslaved wills look helplessly on?

Forgive me if I don't solve that puzzle in the next fifteen minutes. The poet Milton (1608–74) was convinced

that the damned in hell will be debating it for all eternity.
In his imagination, some sat apart, their paradise lost,

> . . . and reasoned high
> Of providence, foreknowledge, will, and fate,
> Fixed fate, free will, foreknowledge absolute,
> And found no end, in wand'ring mazes lost.

Something clearly went wrong. Augustine had no wish to
taunt our impotent wills, or to land us in insoluble para-
doxes; he wished to move us to thanksgiving as the fundamental chord of our being. There may be no way back for
us to Adam and Eve in paradise, beginning each day with
a simple hymn of praise. But, fallen though we are, we can
still ask: What made the leaders of the church insist that
everything we have, without exception, is a gift that summons us to thankfulness?

It may not be easy for us "Anglo-Saxons," as the French
and Germans call us, to understand. Augustine's great adversary Pelagius (d. ca. 419) was British, we are told; and
there is nothing Americans admire more than the self-
made man and the self-made woman, who have relied on
their own shrewdness and industry to get to the top. A recent survey, *What Americans Believe*, found that 82 percent
thought "God helps those who help themselves"; 56 percent believed this to be a quotation from the Bible. It's a
tough world for Augustinians! The Muslims are more
practiced in gratitude than most of us, since they are expected to thank God seventeen times a day. But as Christians, and even as Anglo-Saxons, we can recognize our
debt of gratitude for at least three things.

I

We are thankful *for the gift of life itself.* Our conception
and birth, plainly, are not matters on which we were asked
to vote. In this, if in nothing else, we don't make ourselves,
but receive our self from others.

Some years ago, a friend and colleague of mine who is
an expert on medical ethics was invited to read a paper at
a theological gathering. He agreed, on condition that his

critic would be a medical man, not a theologian like himself, and he suggested the dean of a prominent medical school. When the paper had been read, the physician stood up and began by insisting that he was not a religious man. He then went on to say that to him life was a precious gift to be cherished and nurtured, in ourselves and in others. It was an eloquent and moving confession of a view of life that must lead many a person into the medical profession. And as he spoke, I thought: How close this man's unbelief is to my religion! It was his sense of the sheer gift of human existence that motivated him in his vocation as a doctor, and he found that it challenged him to put first the care of human life and health.

There is, of course, a shadow side to the gift of life. Another professed unbeliever, the Roman poet Lucretius (c. 99–55 B.C.E.), put it succinctly when he wrote that life is given to no one to keep, to all for use—leasehold, not freehold. And sometimes the shortness of life silences our gratitude. But it doesn't have to. A good friend told me how much she looked forward to her husband's retirement, when they would have more time for each other. He died just a few weeks later. I presumed to offer her my sympathies, and there was a note of rebuke in her reply: "I am thankful for the forty years we had."

The time is always short. Sometimes it's shorter than you thought. So, live a little harder, and be grateful for the precious gift of life.

II

We are thankful, too, *for the opportunities life brings us.* In every field of endeavor we value high achievement, and we expect the high achievers to take satisfaction in what hard work has brought them. We congratulate them, and if they are our own family, friends, or students, we can't conceal the special pride their success brings to ourselves. But God alone creates ex nihilo, "out of nothing." For us mortals, creativeness is always treasuring what we receive, questioning it, and passing it on by making of it (we hope) something better.

One of the reasons the story of the ancient Israelites remains so instructive to us is that they learned to receive life's opportunities as so many gifts of God. It may be something of a hyperbole to call their promised land a "land flowing with milk and honey," but Abraham's offspring heard their God saying to them: "I gave you a land on which you had not labored, and towns that you had not built, and you live in them; you eat the fruit of vineyards and olive yards that you did not plant. Now therefore revere the LORD, and serve him in sincerity and in faithfulness" (Josh. 24:13–14). It is easy to make the application to our own lives and opportunities: We work in labs and libraries and classrooms that we did not build; we worship in a magnificent chapel that was there long before we arrived.

Here, again, we have to admit that thankfulness has its shadow side. For how do you suppose the Amorites must have felt, whose land was taken away from them to make room for the Hebrews? And aren't we ourselves more willing to admit these days that many of our best opportunities are not just a sign of God's blessing, but the fruits of human exploitation as well? Anyone from the third world will be ready to show us how this is true—or ask a militant socialist in our own Western world. One person's gratitude is another's resentment. And if thankfulness is not to become complacency, its moral point must be kept constantly before us: which is, responsibility.

Paul's question, "What do you have that you did not receive?" belongs with what he says later about the use of God's gifts for the common good (in 1 Corinthians 12). There are many different gifts, but only one body. The members that appear to be weaker are just as indispensable as the strong, and if one suffers, all suffer. "To each is given the manifestation of the Spirit for the common good" (1 Cor. 12:7).

Real life is a delicate balance between receiving and achieving. None of us is the lone master of his or her destiny, as 82 percent of Americans imagine; but neither are we passive spectators of a drama ordained for us by God, as the predestinarian doctors sometimes appear to

be saying. We receive what we have, and we make ourselves what we are. The difficulty is to affirm both at once.
And if, as an incurable theologian, I venture to say that receiving is the profounder truth, it is because it leads more
readily into the sense of our responsibility for the common good. Our thanks, in the end, can be returned only
to God, the fountain of all good; but thankfulness turns us
toward others, including the others we depend on more
than we like to admit. And that brings me to my last point.

III

We are thankful, above all, *for the healing grace that can
bind up old wounds in the body.* To recognize that the church
at Corinth is an image of humanity is a good first step; to
recognize that things in the church at Corinth had gone
terribly wrong is the crucial second step. The body was divided, dismembered, injured, and diseased, and so is the
human community it mirrors. Those who want to sit in
the seat of the scornful may smile, if they like, at all the
old theological talk about "original sin," "total depravity,"
and the like. But our existence really is broken existence,
and our life together has gone awry. We need the power
of healing grace. It is this need, more than anything else,
that brings us to church and the Lord's Table.

One of the names by which the central act of our Christian worship is known is "Eucharist," which means "gratitude," "thankfulness," or "the act of giving thanks." It is
in receiving the gifts of bread and wine that our wounded
vision is healed and we understand our life together as a
precious gift. Authentic humanity is eucharistic humanity;
or, if you prefer, to be a real person is to be thankful.

If we must speak even here of a shadow side, it lies in
the fact that the bread of the Eucharist points us to a
body broken that we ourselves might be made whole—
one body. "Take, eat; this is my body" (Matt. 26:26).
There is nothing to be done but to receive. Here at the
Lord's Table, if anywhere, you can join Paul and Augustine in their confession: "What do [we] have that [we]
did not receive?"

Hindrances

Truth from the Road

"We must work the works of him who sent me while it is day; night is coming when no one can work."
John 9:4

I happened to be in Britain last July when David Jenkins, a well-known professor of theology, was made Bishop of Durham (6 July 1984). The case of Dr. Jenkins attracted a great deal of attention in the American press, and you may have read about it. He was consecrated in the venerable York Minster amid rumors of heresy, even of blasphemy, because he had told a television audience, some three months earlier, that a modern Christian need not take everything in the ancient creeds too literally. The dignified service was twice interrupted; at one point, a demonstrator briefly took over the lectern until dragged off by security guards. And then, three days later—the very next day after the Archbishop of York had preached in defense of his Durham appointment—the cathedral was struck by lightning.

I

Now, the statistics show that the English are not much inclined to go to church these days, but they still love a good theological controversy, especially if a bishop of the established church is involved. The newspapers, including the *Times* of London, were peppered with columns, letters, and editorials arguing either that the lightning bolt was, or that it was not, a sign of heavenly displeasure with the consecration of Dr. Jenkins.

Others doubted whether the blaze had been caused by lightning at all. Arson was an alternative explanation,

since once before (in 1829) a mad arsonist had tried to
burn the minster down. The Archbishop of Canterbury,
Dr. Runcie, had no explanation of why the fire started; but
he agreed with the fire chief that God was "on our side,"
for while the thirteenth-century wooden roof was consumed, the rose window was spared. The damage could
have been a lot worse. And a laconic note from the cathedral chapter reassured everyone that the building was
insured against such acts of God, anyway—a very impressive testimony to the modernization of faith! The children
of this world are no longer wiser in their generation than
the children of light (cf. Luke 16:8).

Unbelievers, I need hardly add, enjoyed a field day.
That amiable agnostic Conor Cruise O'Brien told the
readers of the *Observer* that while the timing of the lightning bolt was impressive, he could not believe the fire-
from-heaven hypothesis. *One* bolt of lightning may be set
aside as a coincidence. He added, however, that he would
think again if *every time* Dr. Jenkins preached, the church
he preached in were to be struck by lightning.

The profoundest comment I ran across in this otherwise dizzy controversy came from Dr. Habgood, the
Archbishop of York: This is just the kind of thinking (he
said) that the gospel was intended to put an end to. He
didn't say—at least, not in the report I read—what kind of
thinking he had in mind, or what gospel. But we should
have no difficulty working it out for ourselves. And in so
doing we will find ourselves carried beyond this storm in
an English teacup to the heart of our faith in Jesus Christ.

II

What kind of thinking? Well, the kind that imagines
sin and adversity to be always related as cause and effect,
so that if we observe the one, we should look for the other.
Wherever, in this view, we see human failure, we can confidently predict divine judgment; and wherever we witness pain or disaster, or experience them ourselves, there
is some fault to uncover that made them happen.

It is a kind of thinking that takes every hurt and every

tragedy as a punitive act of God, who is assumed to mete out retribution in exact proportion to our guilt. Sin and punishment thus explain accidents and suffering.

Luke the Physician observed this habit of thought among the friendly natives of Malta, when he and the Apostle Paul were shipwrecked on their shores. (With Hellenic condescension, Luke calls the natives "barbarians.") They lit a fire to welcome their uninvited guests, to warm them against the cold and the rain. And as Paul himself gathered a bundle of sticks and placed them on the flames, a poisonous snake came out and wound itself around his hand. The natives immediately concluded he must be a criminal, a murderer; he had escaped from the sea, but divine justice had not allowed him to live. They watched him shake the creature off into the fire, and waited for him to swell up or drop dead. When no misfortune befell him, they changed their minds and said he was a god.

A snakebite observed (or imagined), divine vengeance inferred! It is impossible to read the story as Luke recalls it (in Acts 28) and not to feel that he smiled at the inference, finding it no less superstitious than the change of mind that led the natives to identify Paul as a god. Luke says the snake was "driven out by the heat"—a much simpler explanation, worthy of our modern agnostics.

But sometimes misfortune does strike, and the inference from pain to guilt is no smiling matter. A teenager is totally paralyzed in a car crash, unable even to talk, and the distraught parents ask their pastor: What have we done to deserve this? A young mother gives birth to a baby that has brain damage and is physically deformed, and the grandmother rejects them both with the judgment: "You must have done something terrible, or God would not have punished you this way." And to the agony of physical affliction is added the agony of guilt—or of anger with God, or of a lost faith in God.

Surely, our world makes little sense if we try to force it to fit the narrow dogma that there is an exact proportion between suffering and guilt. Armed with the dogma of retribution, how would you explain the fact that the Lisbon earthquake (1755) struck on All Saints' Day at exactly the hour when the devout were crowded in church to honor the dead? And how would you square the dogma with Job's question:

> Why do the wicked live on,
>   reach old age, and grow mighty in power?
> . . . .
> [While] another dies in bitterness of soul,
>   never having tasted of good?   (Job 21:7, 25)

III

And what does the gospel say that puts an end to this kind of thinking? We might begin with the Gospel of Luke, chapter 13. Jesus is on his way from Galilee to Jerusalem when he is told of some Galilean pilgrims who had gone up to Jerusalem before him, to worship at the Temple. Pilate suspected them of insurrection, sent in troops to disperse them, and so mixed their blood with the blood of their sacrifices.

Do you imagine, Jesus replies, that these Galileans were worse sinners than any other Galileans, because of what they suffered? And he adds another report. A tower in Siloam had fallen on eighteen victims and crushed them. Perhaps they were workers, building defenses or an aqueduct; or perhaps they were handicapped persons, waiting to step into the healing waters of the pool of Siloam. Whoever they were, they were killed. And Jesus' question is the same: Do you imagine that the tower selected the worst offenders to fall on?

Jerusalemites are no safer from accidents than Galileans, and those who suffer disaster are not necessarily more deserving of it than those who are spared. No, accidents do not prove that their victims are more wicked than us; but they do remind us all that life is short and unpredictable, and that we do not have long to repent—to change our thinking and our lives.

Or, we might look more closely at the Gospel of John, chapter 9, which carries the point an important step farther. As Jesus passes by, he notices a man blind from birth.

The disciples see him, too, but quite differently: They see him as a theological puzzle. For if every accident and all suffering are punishments for sin, whose sin can explain a blindness not acquired but congenital?

Here, if ever, is a fact that resists incorporation into the dogma of retribution! If we say that the parents must have sinned, what becomes of the principle: "The wickedness of the wicked shall be his own" (Ezek. 18:20)? But if we say instead that the blind man himself must somehow have sinned before he was born, we are carried off into wholly speculative ideas about prenatal sin, or even about preexistence, rebirth, the transmigration of souls. We will have to rest one weak dogma on another. A perfect theological dilemma!

How does Jesus answer? In a way, he refuses to answer, rejecting the terms of the question, or, if you like, rejecting the dogma it rests on. And he has no other simple hypothesis to put in its place. He dismisses both alternatives: neither the blind man nor his parents sinned. The point, rather, is "that God's works might be revealed in him." The Savior sees the blind man with quite other eyes than the disciples did—not with curiosity or perplexity, but with compassion and assurance of his own mission. And he turns their thoughts from past causes to the present task, taking them up into his appointed work, which is not to solve the riddle of suffering but to be the agent of God's healing power. "We must work the works of him who sent me while it is day; night is coming when no one can work."

Suffering and disaster, we learn, are not so much topics for our discussion as opportunities for our action! We ask for an explanation, and are given an assignment. In this way, even the evil we can't explain becomes an occasion for making manifest the works of God. In the end, we don't invoke the name of God to *explain* the cruelty of humans to humans, or the industrial accident, or the natural catastrophe, or the congenital disease; we invoke it because we have resolved to *do* what we can about them—with every means God makes available to us. Just what we can do, we never know in advance. Sometimes, it is no more than Job's friends did before they unwisely tried to explain his afflictions to him: they sat with him, without a word, "for they saw that his suffering was very great" (Job 2:13).

IV

Many Christians have had their faith shaken in recent times by almost-daily reports of massive starvation, sickness, and death in Africa. The affliction of uncounted thousands is made all the more bitter by persistent rumors that governments have played politics with it, and fraudulent relief agencies have used it for profit. We say we believe in a beneficent and powerful deity who holds the world with loving care. But is it true?

The answer of Jesus is the same today as it was back then: "We must work the works of him who sent me while it is day."

John Mackay, of Princeton, spent many a warm summer's evening on the balcony of a Spanish home, gazing down on the street below. And it dawned on him that here are the two ways by which we attain truth. The balcony is the symbol of "the perfect spectator, for whom life and the universe are permanent objects of study and contemplation." You can learn a great deal by living "a permanently balconized existence." But there are some truths that are not learned through curiosity and observation but through concern, commitment, and action. They are learned as I descend from the balcony to the road, or am thrown onto the road by circumstances.

What Jesus offered his disciples in the words of our text was truth from the road—a faith that was not an explanation, but obedience. That is what he still offers. We crave assurance of God, in spite of everything, and it comes to us—totally unexpectedly—in the call to do God's work. No further argument is needed to reinforce the call, and no argument can stop us from hearing it. However it may be in other departments of learning, here, at least, the principle holds true: The one who does, knows (see John 7:17).

Evil at the Hand of God?

"Shall we receive good at the hand of God,
and shall we not receive evil?"

Job 2:10

A former next-door neighbor of mine was an avid football fan who liked to follow the "Irish"; if I remember rightly, he was a Notre Dame alumnus. But in the south suburbs of Chicago, where I then lived, it isn't usually possible to pick up the "away" games live on television from South Bend. He solved the problem one summer when I was on vacation. I came back to find an enormous antenna towering over my two-story home. I should think it must have been capable of picking up any Big Ten game within a five-hundred-mile radius. It was like living next door to the state police; only the flashing red light that warns off friendly aircraft was missing.

Seeing that I was a bit apprehensive, my neighbor pointed out all the fine features of his new antenna. It was sunk deep in concrete, and he demonstrated the sturdiness of the metal frame by climbing up it for me. This, I grant, was impressive, because he had a linebacker's physique that had spread out with advancing years. So I was not particularly anxious when he moved and left his antenna standing. But it fell.

During a windstorm it fell on the front of my house, buckling the gutters, and then crashed through my favorite evergreen onto the lawn. Now, my lawn was not a suburban showpiece, I must admit (I'd been meaning to do something about it for years); and my new neighbor's wife pointed out helpfully that the antenna could have fallen on one of my children. "Somebody up there," she said, "is watching over us." Forgetting that we are both

Presbyterians, I answered as only a theologian could: "Then why didn't that Somebody stop it from falling on my gutters?"

The insurance agent was theologically of the same persuasion as my neighbor's wife: what had happened, he explained, was an act of God, and therefore he was sorry, but his company could not assume financial liability. When a repairman came, however, he attributed the fall to metal deterioration plus the force of the wind: he didn't mention the activity of God. And yet my neighbors did not contest his explanation, nor did anyone else. So you may well wonder: What exactly *did* God do? What, indeed, *does* God do?

I

How clearly our everyday language betrays the limits of our faith! We invoke the name of God chiefly on special occasions. To account for an accident: "It was an act of God," we say. Or to breathe our sigh of relief at some narrow escape: "Somebody up there is watching over us." Or to guarantee our escape in advance: "Spare me, and I'll never drink another drop." Or to shrug off our accountability: "I can't help the way the good Lord made me." Or to admit that we've tried everything else and have come to the end of our resources: "Now it's in the hands of God"—as though it were not in God's hands from the beginning! One way or another, we parcel out the course of our existence, dividing it up between God and other causes; and it's the other causes—like metal fatigue and the force of the wind—that we talk about most of the time.

On reflection, we may decide that a sound instinct lies behind our unreflective habits of speech: the fact is that there are some things we would rather *not* attribute to God. After three operations in a terribly short life, a seven-month-old baby girl dies of liver disease, because she never put on enough weight to tolerate a transplant. Her disease (biliary atresia) afflicts only one in twenty-five thousand. Do we really want to say that God gave it to her? We would gladly believe that this one time something went wrong with the Creator's handiwork, that the clay slipped in the potter's hands.

A young man is critically injured waterskiing, and he survives only because his companion is a medical student and knows how to keep him alive. But he survives as a quadriplegic who wishes he had died. Did God do that? Or dare we ascribe to God the crash of the jumbo jet that takes 275 lives (the DC-10 at O'Hare, 1979), or the earthquake that with supreme irony brings the roof of the church down on the heads of the worshipers (Italy, 1980)?

It helps, up to a point, when we can recognize the role of human folly or malice in the occurrence of disaster. Remove the brush from the hillside to prevent fires, and you risk a mudslide instead. Disregard proper maintenance procedures, and the responsibility for the crash must surely be laid at *your* door. Negligence takes hundreds of lives every year: to tell the bereaved it was God's will, though you mean well, may only add to the pain. And it is human depravity that accounts for the looters who profit from disaster, for the shopkeepers who raise their prices, and for the relief workers who pilfer the supplies. Why should we blame God?

But nobody pretends that human perversity can *always* take *all* the blame. Why did the earthquake happen to begin with, making the relief work necessary? Do both human depravity and the course of nature lie outside God's control? This is the conclusion Rabbi Harold Kushner arrived at in his best-seller *When Bad Things Happen to Good People*. His son Aaron was found to have the terrible affliction (progeria) that accelerates a child's aging process: he died at the age of fourteen, with the body of a little old man.

In his grief, Rabbi Kushner was able to save his belief in the infinite goodness of God only by surrendering belief in God's omnipotence: there must be accidents, he concluded, that God doesn't intend.

> God can't do everything [he says]. . . . I don't believe
> God causes mental retardation in children, or chooses
> who should suffer from muscular dystrophy. The God
> I believe in does not send us the problem. . . . Fate, not
> God, sends us the problem.

Thousands of perplexed sufferers and mourners have been saved by the rabbi's message from giving up their faith in the goodness of God. But they pay a price when they surrender the infinite power of God. And Job's question doesn't go away: "Shall we receive good at the hand of God, and shall we not receive evil?"

II

Others who have suffered and reflected on suffering have arrived at exactly the opposite conclusion to Rabbi Kushner's: God is always in control but God isn't always fair, nor even (in any ordinary sense of the word) always good. A young woman, both of her children terminally afflicted with a rare and incurable blood disease, says: "I believe God's in control of everything. If I didn't believe that, I wouldn't get up in the morning."

A young minister, stricken with multiple sclerosis and confined to a wheelchair, has to struggle with the irony that God seems to hinder his ministry. In retrospect, he says: "My theological reasoning goes something like this: I've decided to preserve God's sovereignty at the expense of divine goodness. It's more important to believe God is in control than to believe God is good in every way. I think we have to face the fact that God isn't fair."

Stern theology indeed! One thinks of a favorite text of Martin Luther (1483–1546):

> There is no God beside me.
> I kill and I make alive;
>   I wound and I heal;
> and no one can deliver from my hand.
>   (Deut. 32:39)

At first, those terrible words appall us, and we may be inclined to dismiss them as belonging to an earlier stage of revelation, now happily left behind us. But Luther's profound thought is by no means to be dismissed. He did not mean that God does both good things and bad things, but that sometimes God brings good out of bad: he slays and makes alive at the same time, giving life by putting to death. And I think Luther had experience on his side.

Every Christian minister can attest that there is no direct proportion between the quantity of a person's health, wealth, or wisdom and the quantity of his or her faith in God. The deepest faith is often to be found along with the deepest affliction. And for many, the purest comfort is precisely that every affliction comes from the hand of God. This it is that preserves their faith from crumbling at the very first onslaught of life's negative experiences. To the question: How can they affirm their faith in the teeth of what looks to us like irrefutable counterevidence? they reply that they never learned to trust God fully until they bowed before this truth: that it is God, and no other, who both slays and makes alive, both wounds and heals.

But perhaps they too pay a price. They cannot always *see* that God brings good out of bad, and apparently senseless evil—too intense or too extensive to assimilate—can only evoke a kind of stoic resignation. And this may be the way we should take Job's question to his wife: "Shall we receive good at the hand of God, and shall we not receive evil?"

III

Although I do have my own thoughts on the subject, it is not now my intention to adjudicate between these two approaches to the problem of evil, or to offer any third alternative. Any thoughtful believer can learn from both. And while the two appear to be sharply opposed—the one curtailing God's infinite power and the other God's infinite goodness—the essential truth is the same in both. Whether God causes evil, or evil is simply outside divine control, the heart of the matter is this: that God is not our adversary, not our accuser, but is on our side.

Evil has done its worst when I infer that God is against me, and I ask: Why me? What have I done? And my guilt torments me. But this is to imagine that I am justified by works. The profound truth that the Apostle Paul affirms in our New Testament lesson (Romans 8) is that providence and evil are rightly grasped only by those who are justified by faith. For to be justified by faith is nothing other than to know that, despite everything, God in Christ is *for* us. It is God who justifies! And if God is for us, who—or what—can be against us (v. 31)?

Here is the foundation of Paul's confident words: "We know that in everything God works for good with those who love him" (v. 28, RSV). The cynics ask "Can God tie a knot that he cannot untie?" and think they have disproved omnipotence. But that's not what we mean by "omnipotence"—that God can do *anything*. We mean, with Paul, that the love of God in Christ Jesus is everywhere powerfully at work, that there is no situation it cannot reach, and that nothing can separate us from it.

That, surely, is the answer to the question with which we began: What does God *do?* God works unceasingly for good with those who love the Lord, "who are called according to his purpose" (Rom. 8:28). And for us, whatever Job may have meant, to receive evil at the hand of God is not necessarily to say that God inflicted it, but to look for the hand of divine love even there. We don't pretend it is always easy. But Paul attests that it is possible, because the call is "to be conformed to the image of [God's] Son" (v. 29), who was not spared but given up to the cross for us all (v. 32).

The View from Eternity

*"He has made everything beautiful in its time;
also he has put eternity into [the human] mind,
yet so that [they] cannot find out what God has
done from the beginning to the end."*
                                        Ecclesiastes 3:11

To announce such a text as this takes more than a
preacher's usual folly. To begin with, Ecclesiastes is a
problem book, and many have doubted whether it belongs
in our Bible. The title it bears in the RSV, "Ecclesiastes,
Or the Preacher," hardly reflects the nameless author's
style. We might better call him "the Philosopher." He was
not a prophet burdened with a word from the Lord, but a
sage—a wise man reflecting on his own experience.

His perspective is earthly: "I . . . applied my mind to
seek and to search out by wisdom all that is done under
heaven" (1:12–13). And his conclusion is bleak: "I saw all
the deeds that are done under the sun; and see, all is vanity and a chasing after wind" (1:14). Even his pursuit of
learning wearies him, for "those who increase knowledge
increase sorrow" (1:18). The most positive thing he can
find to say is that there is some fleeting satisfaction in
work. But it's not going to get us anywhere: the grave is
the common destiny of us all, the wise and the fools alike
(2:16).

The Philosopher made it into the Old Testament because he was mistakenly supposed to have been the wise
King Solomon. An unlikely supposition, to say the least!
His weariness of life (2:17) and his skepticism are out of
keeping with the rest of our Bible. But if there is always a
little doubt mixed in with our faith, and some tiredness

mixed in with our zest for life, we may be glad of the honesty that placed Ecclesiastes in the midst of our sacred Scriptures. Even John Calvin (1509–64), who had an enviable assurance most of the time, could write: "While we teach that faith ought to be certain and assured, we cannot imagine any certainty that is not tinged with doubt, or any assurance that is not assailed by some anxiety."

But then there's the special difficulty of my chosen text. If one were to name the most problematic verse in this problematic book, it would have to be chapter 3, verse 11. To mention only the biggest difficulty of all: What is it that God has put into the human mind? The old King James Version says: "He hath set the world in their heart." The Revised Standard Version says: "He has put eternity into man's mind." The commentaries tell us that the Hebrew word, with only a slight change, could be translated "mystery," "enigma," "ignorance," or "forgetfulness"; but also the direct opposite of ignorance, "knowledge." Then again it could mean "toil" or "work." And these are not the only possibilities. How such diverse—even directly opposed—meanings could be given to a single word, only a Hebrew scholar can say. And even the scholars may finally raise their hands in surrender and ask with the Philosopher: "Who is like the wise man?/And who knows the interpretation of a thing?" (8:1).

Still, my text is—to me—one of those irresistibly fascinating sayings that, once we have begun to think about them, we cannot leave alone. As Ecclesiastes itself so rightly tells us, "The sayings of the wise are like goads" (12:11)—they spur us on to thought. I can only share my own thoughts with you, and invite you to think *with* me— to hope and to trust that there is a word of God for us in this intriguing, enigmatic text.

I simply take the verse, without further ado, more or less in the form given it by the Revised Standard Version—the form in which it first captured my interest. For the rest, I borrow the disarming words of the old Scots Confession and ask, "if anyone should note in this [my] confession any article or sentence repugnant to God's holy word, that it would please them of their gentleness, and for Christian charity's sake, to admonish [me] of the same in writing."

I

"He has made everything beautiful in its time." The text falls naturally into three parts. The first sums up the powerful and moving verses, 1–8, that were read in our Old Testament lesson: "For everything there is a season, and a time for every matter under heaven: a time to be born, and a time to die. . . ." And so on, down to "a time for war, and a time for peace." Maybe one should rest content with the reading of this elegant, rhythmic discourse, and should not risk spoiling it with explanations. But let's ask at least this much: Why does the Philosopher want us to note that everything is beautiful in its time?

Most commentators explain that he means to teach us our powerlessness to change the irresistible necessity that governs our entire existence. Everything happens as fore-ordained, at exactly the time appointed for it, and none of us can change the predestined pattern of our lives. Each event in our outward and our inward lives is unalterably fixed, even the emotions of our hearts.

But I don't see how that can be the whole of the Philosopher's message. He tells us that "the wise mind will *know* the time and way. For every matter has its time and way" (8:5–6). This, surely, can only be an exhortation to be watchful and to seize the right moment for action, not simply to resign ourselves to what we cannot change. When opportunity knocks, we must be ready to open the door, since there may not be another time.

Of course, there are some things in which we have no choice. You can't pick the time to be born. Neither, as a rule, can you decide when you will die. As the Philosopher says, like a fish taken in an evil net, or a bird caught in a snare, you may find that your time comes suddenly (9:12). But you can, for instance, rejoice in your youth while you are young; and you should, because childhood and youth are fleeting (11:9; 12:1). Not resignation only, but watch-fulness too is the message of Ecclesiastes. And the peace

of calm acceptance. Otherwise, why does he say that
everything is *beautiful* in its time?

He knows that even death has no terrors for one who
can affirm that there is a time to die, to let go one's hold
on life itself. At the age of seventy-one, the great philosopher Immanuel Kant (1724–1804) could still write his
noble essay on eternal peace. But then, we are told, he was
exhausted. "One by one his sensibilities and his powers
left him; and in 1804, aged seventy-nine, he died, quietly
and naturally, like a leaf falling from a tree."

"He has made everything beautiful in its time." If we
ask: What is it that enables us to accept life's negative
events and even the surrender of life itself? the answer
must be that we see them as pieces that fit into a larger
pattern. And this may be the way to interpret the second
part of my text.

II

"He has put eternity into [the human] mind." We can
honestly say that everything has its time only if we have
somehow won a larger perspective, a higher vantage
point. If the sum total of our times under the sun add up,
then we can see the beauty in the part because we discover
its fit within the whole. We take the view from eternity.
Whatever else "eternity" may mean, we can think of it as
comprehensive time, in which the fragments of time are
gathered up into a larger scheme of things; and each fleeting moment then has significance as it is brought to the
light of eternity in this sense.

Some years ago, a good friend of mine was dying of
stomach cancer. I hadn't seen him for a while; and when
I was ushered into his room, my face must have uninten-
tionally shown my shock at his emaciated, ravaged body.
To my astonishment, he responded with a smile that was
not just cordial, but even a little bit mocking, and he said
simply: "The Lord has been very good to me." I knew I
was being gently rebuked. And as he began to reminisce,
I realized what enabled him to be at peace. I saw only the
time of suffering; he saw his life as a whole—from the

beginning to its approaching end—and the God he had known from childhood didn't desert him in his time of greatest need. His death brought him closer to eternity.

Enlarge that sense of wholeness to include, not your own life only, but also the lives of others in the one human epic, and you have the view from eternity, no longer the view from under the sun. You can put things in their place, see them in proportion. Indeed, to view all our times in the light of eternity is perhaps as good a definition of being religious as there is. It is not enough for us to believe that each and every thing that happens under the sun is divinely ordained. We are driven by a kind of instinct to get beyond our fragmentary times, and to see them all as parts of one design. This, I believe, is what it must mean to say that God has put "eternity"—comprehensive time—into the human mind or heart.

A preacher could not preach at all if she or he were not persuaded that, deep down, this is what brings us all to church. Of course, we can always run away from eternity, immerse ourselves in the present moment and rush on to the next. We can ask not to be bothered or disturbed with thoughts of eternity, and can demand instead to be given wise advice for the problem of the moment, whatever it happens to be. But in the end we want to make sense of our life and of our world; the view from eternity is finally what we want.

There is, of course, a difficulty, however. The view from eternity is strictly God's view, while we must lead our lives, with the Philosopher, under the heavens. Which brings me to the third part of my text. God has put eternity into the human mind—

III

". . . yet so that they cannot find out what God has done from the beginning to the end." It is easy to understand why many of the Philosopher's interpreters cannot believe that he meant "eternity" at all. If, they say, we cannot find out what God has done from the beginning to the end, then God must have put, not eternity, but mystery or ignorance or an enigma into our minds, so that we search in vain for the grand design in the march of events.

I don't suppose that the meaning of the words in my text will ever be settled by linguistics alone. I can only say that it doesn't seem to me to follow logically that because the cosmic pattern partly eludes us, therefore God cannot have put the longing for it in our minds. The confession of the devout believer, even as he or she reaches for the meaning of the whole, is this: "Now I only know in part; then I will know fully, even as I have been fully known" (1 Cor. 13:12). We live by as much of the pattern as we *can* see, and we are constantly reaching out for *more*.

All of us can point to events that, however hard we try, we cannot fit into our vision of God's plan: events that seem totally cruel or senseless. The well-intentioned solutions of even the wisest among us then seem trivial and unconvincing, even irritatingly complacent. G. W. Leibniz (1646–1716) asks with a rhetorical flourish: "Is it not most often necessary that a little evil render the good more discernible?" And we want to reply: Yes, but what's the use of a lot of evil, if a little would do? There is a time for explanations—and there is a time just to weep. Our intimations of eternity don't take away the mystery of our existence. We don't claim that they do; we admit, with Ecclesiastes, that "God is in heaven, and [we] upon earth," so that our words should be few (Eccl. 5:2).

This, then, is what I take my text to mean. God has put eternity into the human mind, yet so that we cannot know it all. To be human is to be caught between glimpses of eternity and the acceptance of enigma. Without eternity, we might be contented animals; without the enigma, we would be omniscient gods. This is by no means a message out of harmony with the rest of our Bible. The faith of the New Testament doesn't contradict it, but illustrates and confirms it.

In Jerusalem, some 250 years after Ecclesiastes was written, a young preacher was charged with blasphemy and treason, and was executed by crucifixion. Deserted by his band of followers, he felt himself deserted by God (Mark 14:50; 15:34). Those who sat down and watched him there (Matt. 27:36) could only have seen a young man cut off uselessly in the prime of life, though it was said of him that he had done nothing wrong (Luke 23:41). Hard to fit into anyone's cosmic plan! But how different the view from eternity contained in the first chapter of the Letter to the Ephesians!

The pieces fall into place in a single pattern, with the crucified one at the center. His coming was in the fullness of time, and it imparts insight into the divine plan, the mystery of God's will (Eph. 1:9–10). And yet the author of the letter must still pray for his readers that the Father of glory would enlighten the "eyes of [their] heart" and give them "a spirit of wisdom and revelation as [they] come to know [God]" (vv. 17–18). Almost two millennia later, we venture to ask the same spirit for ourselves.

The Lightbearer

"Many Infallible Proofs"

(Easter Sunday)

*"To them he presented himself alive
after his passion by many proofs."*

Acts 1:3

Easter, like Christmas, is a time for retelling a treasured story, and a time for celebration in music and song. The story comes to us in more than one version. But the heart of them all is this: that death and burial did not close the final chapter in the life of Jesus; that by some mysterious act of God he was seen alive again three days later; and that the astonishing news lifted the weary band of his dejected disciples out of despair into new hope and confidence.

The story has its meaning not for them only, but for all of us who call ourselves by Christ's name. The mystery of our salvation is that we are baptized into his death, so that we too might "walk in newness of life" (Rom. 6:4). The gospel of Jesus Christ neither reassures us of our in-born virtue nor gives us up for hopeless; it offer us—precisely—new life in Christ. That may come as bad news to those who thought they had done all right with the life they received from their mother's womb. But it is gospel—good news—to those for whom the old life could never satisfy, because what is born of the flesh can never be more than flesh (John 3:6). As Martin Luther (1483–1546) liked to say, "If God makes alive, he does it by putting to death."

Easter faith is confidence in a God who brings new life out of the old. Perhaps there is nothing more to be done on Easter Sunday than to reaffirm this faith—as grateful witnesses of the resurrection, simply to hear the story again and to respond in song:

Jesus Christ is risen today. . . .
. . . .
Hymns of praise then let us sing
Unto Christ, our heavenly King;
Alleluia!

I

Still, anyone who ponders the several versions of the
story is bound to be struck by one constant, disturbing
strain, which may inhibit celebration. Is it true? Did it
really happen—that God raised Jesus from the dead?
Throughout the narratives there is an astonishingly can-
did note of doubt, or at least an admission that it isn't easy
to believe, and this may seem to put in question the very
grounds on which the hope for new life rests.

The Apostle Paul arrives in Athens, home of a prominent university, and mingles with philosophers in the
marketplace. He talks to them about Jesus and *anastasis*,
which means "resurrection." Misunderstanding, they
think he must be introducing two new divinities to them,
and they invite him to give a lecture. For all the Atheni-
ans and visitors to Athens, we are told, spend their time
telling and hearing something new (Acts 17:21). We can
imagine that everything goes well as long as Paul speaks a
language the philosophers can applaud, which he does.
He even quotes winning lines from two familiar poets. But
how is it when he explains the real meaning of *anastasis*:
not the name of a hitherto unknown goddess, but resurrection from death? We read that when his audience hear
about the dead rising again, some laugh; others say they
will hear Paul again—meaning, I take it, some other day,
not today.

There you have the response of sophisticated outsiders.
But that is not all. More surprising, the difficulty of believing the resurrection appeared among Christ's chosen
apostles. "Doubting Thomas," in the Gospel of John, on
hearing that others had seen the risen Lord, retorted that
unless he saw in the Lord's hands the print of the nails, he,
at least, would not believe (20:24). And Thomas was not

the exception. The narratives in Matthew, Mark, and Luke are all, in one sense, a litany of unbelief—or, better, of *slow* belief. The joyful testimony of others that the Lord is alive meets with incredulity: surely, the reports must be idle tales (Luke 24:11; cf. Mark 16:11, 13, 14)! And not all who see the risen Lord for themselves can quite believe it (Matt. 28:17). Some even mistrust their own joy at seeing him, and they are confused. "In their joy they were disbelieving and still wondering" (Luke 24:41).

Robust doubt, nervous mistrust, downright confusion—these are all with us still, in the midst of the Christian community as well as on the outside. While I was in Scotland last fall [1990], the reviews of Piers Paul Read's new novel, *On the Third Day*, began to appear. In it Read imagines what might happen if excavations in Jerusalem positively identified the remains of a crucified man as those of Jesus. In a column in the *Guardian*, he reports that his wife said it would make no difference. But she, he explains, is an agnostic. For himself, to doubt the bodily resurrection of Christ would make nonsense of the Christian religion. And he quotes, as many another will be quoting this morning, the words of the Apostle Paul: "If Christ has not been raised, then our proclamation has been in vain and your faith has been in vain" (1 Cor. 15:14).

But if we agree with Read about the consequences of unbelief in the resurrection, it does not follow that we must consider belief easy: the Gospel record itself, we have seen, is against any such conclusion. And every year, when Easter comes around again, the religious columns in our daily press (as you will have noticed) raise the question: Is it so? Michael Hirsley wrote in the Chicago *Tribune* on March 22: "Despite nonreligious add-ons such as colored eggs, candies and the Easter Bunny, the religious message of Easter is kept clear and simple. But that doesn't mean the message doesn't get complicated and questioned: Did Jesus rise from the dead?"

II

A common response to this nagging question has been to point to the many remarkable testimonies of the New

Testament to Jesus' bodily resurrection. We are told in Acts 1:3 (KJV) that, after his passion, Jesus showed himself alive to his chosen apostles "by many infallible proofs." The Revised Standard Version says just "by many proofs" (leaving out the "infallible"). But the Greek word is a strong one: it really does mean "convincing, demonstrative proof." (That's what it meant to Aristotle [384–322 B.C.E.].) For this reason, I have always liked the phrase in the old King James Version, "many *infallible* proofs." It provided the title (in 1886) for one of the most confident works of Christian apologetics I have ever seen: *"Many Infallible Proofs": The Evidences of Christianity*, by Arthur T. Pierson, minister of Bethany Presbyterian Church in Philadelphia. "These proofs," the author assures us, "if they are candidly examined, will cure all honest doubt."

Strangely, Pierson didn't say much about the resurrection, to which the phrase in Acts refers, although he undertook to prove just about everything else that Christians believe. But many others have taken up the challenge. They have tried to show, in particular, that every attempt to explain away the empty tomb fails. Such explanations are legion. The women looked in the wrong tomb, one that really was empty. Jesus was not dead when they laid him in the grave, but had only passed out, and later revived. The disciples stole the body and pretended that he had risen from the dead. And so on.

I can gladly cheer on our apologists as they seek to overthrow these ingenious, but inept, explanations of two millennia of Christian faith. But experience does not bear out the claim that the many infallible proofs advanced on the other side do, in fact, "cure all honest doubt." And I suspect, in any case, that to focus attention on the empty tomb is to look in the wrong place. We might even venture to take the angel's admonition in this sense: "I know that you are looking for Jesus who was crucified. He is not here" (Matt. 28:5–6).

The proofs don't often win the outsider. This is the point made with mischievous wit in *The Way of All Flesh*, by Samuel Butler (1835–1902). His young hero—whom he names, with pleasant irony, Ernest Pontifex—decides to convert Mr. Shaw, the tinker, who mends the pots and pans downstairs. Ernest runs quickly over his notes on the *Evidences* of William Paley (1743–1805), slips a copy of *Historic Doubts* by Archbishop William Whateley (1583–1639) into his pocket, and is ready for his mission.

Whateley's argument, I should say, is that objections of the same kind as the skeptics bring against Christian miracles would also prove that Napoleon Bonaparte never existed. Ernest eagerly asks Mr. Shaw, who has read the book, what he thinks of it. Mr. Shaw is very civil. Carrying on quietly with his work, he remarks: "I think that he who was so willing and able to prove that what was was not, would be equally able and willing to make a case for thinking that what was not was, if it suited his purpose." Ernest is dumbfounded: he had never learned that rejoinder from anyone at Cambridge. And Mr. Shaw proceeds to get him hopelessly mixed up over the different resurrection narratives in the New Testament. "Now go upstairs," he concludes, "and read the accounts of the Resurrection correctly without mixing them up . . . then if you feel inclined to pay me another visit I shall be glad to see you. . . . Till then, sir, I must wish you a very good morning."

III

It may well be possible to order the many infallible proofs of the empty tomb better than Ernest could. And those who are determined to try are just as much a part of our Christian family as those who believe with no proofs at all. But is there no third alternative? May we look elsewhere for the crucified and risen Lord than in the empty tomb? Surely the stories themselves show us an alternative. Consider, in particular, two familiar recognition narratives.

Mary Magdalene (in John's version [20:1–18]), coming to the tomb early in the morning while it is still dark, sees that the stone has been rolled away. But this by no means leads her to faith in Jesus' resurrection. She thinks the body has been stolen, and runs to tell the others. Later she returns to the tomb, sobbing. This time, she sees the risen Lord standing outside, and supposes him to be the gardener. They talk, but she doesn't recognize him until he addresses her by name, "Mary." The response is immediate: "Master!" She tries to embrace him, but it is not permitted.

The best commentary on this story, with its simple climax in the exchange of two words ("Mary," "Master"), is an earlier discourse in the same Gospel. The sheep hear their shepherd's voice, and he calls them by name (John 10:3). He knows his own, and his own know him (v. 14). Mary was convinced that the Lord was alive, not by seeing his body, but by hearing his word; and his word convinced her only as a wholly personal word addressed to her by name. Is it not the same for all of us? We are convinced that we are in the presence of the living Lord when his word comes home to us as if it had our name on it.

In the second recognition story, besides the word, there is also a tangible proof. Two men (in Luke's account [24:13–35]) are traveling together on the Emmaus road, sadly conversing about all that has happened, and Jesus falls in with them. They do not recognize him when he asks what they were talking about. They do not recognize him even when he explains to them all the Scriptures about himself. Still, they urge him to stay the night with them. And at table, when they are about to eat together, the mysterious stranger takes the bread, and blesses and breaks it, and gives it to them. They recognize him in the breaking of bread, and say to each other: "Were not our hearts burning within us while he was talking to us on the road?" (v. 32). We think, of course, of the Eucharist as we read the climax of this story, and surely we are meant to. The Eucharist is the tangible sign of the Lord's presence, and it brings to our minds all those times when our hearts have burned within us at his words of reassurance and demand, of encouragement and rebuke.

Some years ago, on the occasion of another Easter, a good friend reported to me, with great glee, that one of our best-known evangelists had just spoken with the news media. Asked if he believed Jesus is alive, he had answered: "I know he is: I spoke to him this morning." I was expected to laugh at such naïveté. But, to be honest, I think it was a wiser response than any attempt to prove the tomb was empty, though we might do better to reverse the order of the response. It is not so much that *we* talk to the living Lord, but that *his* Word is addressed to us, and by it he becomes Lord over our lives.

Our doubt dissolves when the word of Christ addresses us, as it did Mary Magdalene. Our doubt dissolves when we are invited, at the Lord's Table, to reach out our hand and receive the signs of the body and blood given for us. And our doubt dissolves when we turn to one another, as we are gathered together, and pass on the greeting of the risen Lord, "Peace be with you" (John 20:19, 26).

Our celebration does not have to wait till all the proofs of the resurrection are in: the celebration brings all the proofs we need. We have as many infallible proofs that Christ lives as there are worshipers in this great church—and there are many more outside and beyond. May his peace be with us all.

The Christ of Faith

*"But I am not ashamed, for I know the one in whom
I have put my trust, and I am sure that he is able to
guard until that day what has been entrusted to me."*
2 Timothy 1:12

"I know the one in whom I have put my trust." The calm assurance of these words is all the more striking when we notice, from the final chapter, that this is a farewell letter—though the author still hopes there may be time to say farewell in person (2 Tim. 4:9, 21). We are to picture him languishing in prison, awaiting martyrdom. "I am already being poured out as a libation, and the time of my departure has come. I have fought the good fight, I have finished the race" (4:6–7). He is now powerless to carry on his holy calling as a missionary of Jesus Christ; it is, indeed, the outspoken exercise of his mission as herald, teacher, and apostle that has brought suffering on him (1:11–12). And he writes to urge his young friend and fellow worker to take his share of suffering for the gospel (1:8). But . . . he is not ashamed! He knows the one in whom he has placed his trust.

He means, I take it, that for all the grim horror that awaits him, at least he has no need to be anxious for the gospel. The one to whom he has entrusted himself is the Savior, Christ Jesus, or the God who has made grace manifest in the Savior's appearing and has brought life and immortality to light through the gospel (1:9–10). The gospel, entrusted though it is to frail humans, is finally in the Savior's own safe hands: he will take care of it.

Now, the scholars tell us it is unlikely that the letter was really, as the church once believed, written by the Apostle Paul as he faced his death. Many of the expressions used are foreign to Paul's language, and some of his most basic thoughts are not there. Very likely, an unknown

author wrote the letter to keep the church faithful to the
Pauline gospel, perhaps using some genuine fragments
from the Apostle's own hand. But the question is not
whether Paul could have said the words of my text; the
question is whether you and I can. What hinders us is a
quite different problem than his.

I

Back in October 1992, a banner headline caught my
eye in a British weekly: "Man and Myth—More Bad News
for Believers." It was a review of several recent attempts
to rescue the real Jesus from the church. The most
provocative of them had already created a sensation in the
public news media, chiefly by its argument that Jesus married Mary Magdalene, had three children with her (two
boys and a girl), divorced her, and was remarried—this
time to the Lydia of whom we read in the Acts of the
Apostles. (Acts 16:14 tells us that "the Lord opened her
[Lydia's] heart," which, being interpreted, must mean
that they fell in love.)

Naturally, this hypothesis assumes that Jesus did not
die on the cross. Poison given him as an act of mercy only
left him unconscious. In the tomb Simon the Magician
(who, we are told, was one of the two offenders crucified
with Jesus) was able to revive him with the spices left by
the women. Jesus lived to a ripe old age, retiring in his sev-
enties to the south of France.

"Total rubbish" was the verdict of one senior New
Testament scholar, and I am willing to believe him. But
the bad news, if there is any, is this: serious scholars are
unable to agree on what *isn't* rubbish. And to some believers, at least, the absence of a scholarly consensus is
deeply disturbing. Volume after volume appears, inviting
us to join the exciting quest for the historical Jesus, and we
are left to decide whether Jesus was a marginal Jew, a
Mediterranean peasant, a wandering Cynic, a revolution-
ary, a Galilean holy man, or what. Can we say anymore
that we know the one in whom we believe? Or are we being invited on an endless, inconclusive quest?

II

In the Gospel lesson (John 12:20–36), we hear of certain Greeks who wanted to see Jesus. The narrative raises a host of questions; we can only make guesses at the answers. Why were Greeks going up to attend the Jewish Passover? Why didn't they go directly to Jesus, instead of making their request to Philip? And what has Jesus' "answer" to do with the request, anyway? We are all accustomed to looking for symbolic meanings in the Fourth Gospel. They are assuredly present here, and they go to the heart of our problem.

At the beginning of the chapter, we learn that six days before the Passover Jesus stayed in Bethany at the home of Lazarus and his sisters, Martha and Mary. A crowd gathered, curious because they heard that Jesus had raised Lazarus from the dead. Many had come to believe in him. The next day was the occasion of Jesus' triumphal entry into Jerusalem, accompanied by a chorus of loud hosannas. Once again John explains that the crowd ran to greet him because they had learned about the raising of Lazarus. Disgruntled, the Pharisees remark that the whole world is going after him.

The whole world? That sounds like an exaggeration, born out of resentment. ("You see," the Pharisees say, "you can do nothing." It seems impossible to stop Jesus' triumphal progress. The whole world is going after him.) But the account has said only that many of *the Jews* were going away and believing in Jesus (v. 11). The way John speaks of "the Jews" is often an embarrassment to us, seeing that Jesus himself and his disciples were Jewish. But here it has a point. The mission of Jesus is to "the lost sheep of the house of Israel" (Matt. 15:24; cf. Matt. 10:5). Would it be fair to take the children's food and throw it to the dogs (Mark 7:27; Matt. 15:26)? John does not record this harsh saying of Jesus, but in its light we can readily understand the request of the Greeks: they are outsiders, hesitant to push themselves forward. How can *they* come to Jesus?

"Sir, *we* wish to see Jesus"—the Greeks, too. They

stand for the other half of the world, which also yearns for the Redeemer. And the difficulty is that the rest of the world has no immediate access to him. They can only approach indirectly—through the retinue of his apostles. It is no accident that John mentions Philip, whose name is Greek (it means "lover of horses"). Philip tells Andrew—another Greek name ("manly"). But both are Jewish; they provide the link between the Jewish Messiah and the Gentile world.

The narrative gives us no reason at all to think that the Greeks ever did get to see Jesus. Rather, Philip and Andrew report to Jesus, and his answer to them seems hardly to be an answer, even indirectly, to the Greeks. He gives a discourse on life through death! Some commentators argue that there is no connection with the request of the Greeks—just the introduction of another fragment of Jesus' story. Others suggest that the theme of life through death is in fact an answer to the Greeks, whose ideal was self-cultivation, not self-sacrifice. Jesus, in that case, would be throwing down a challenge to the Greek view of life.

But surely, if we take our entire Gospel lesson as a unity, the point is given in verse 32: ". . . and I, *when I am lifted up from the earth*, will draw all people to myself." The evangelist comments: "He said this to indicate the kind of death he was to die"—that is, crucifixion. And this is the answer to the Greeks. Only when he has been raised up on his cross will the rest of the world "see Jesus." The Greeks must wait.

John's meaning, then, is that *from the cross* Christ will draw persons of every race and nation to himself. The simile for this paradoxical truth is the grain of wheat that remains "just a single grain" unless it is buried in the ground and "dies." Its fruitfulness is its apparent dissolution. Just so, only by the sacrifice of his bodily existence could the work of the Savior be freed from its natural human limitations. His earthly life is but the seed of his glory as Lord. And believing in him may call for a similar readiness on the part of his followers to suffer loss for the sake of life.

The crowd objects on behalf of Jesus' own country-
men: According to the law, the Messiah remains forever.
The answer to *them*, who do have access to the earthly
Jesus, is this: "The light is with you for a little longer. . . .
While you have the light, believe in the light" (vv. 35–36).
The meaning, clearly, is that the light is about to be passed
on, and our thoughts go back to Yahweh's servant in the
prophecy of Isaiah. The Lord says:

> "It is too light a thing that you should be my servant
>   to raise up the tribes of Jacob
>   and to restore the survivors of Israel;
> I will give you as a light to the nations,
>   that my salvation may reach to the end of the
>   earth."   (Isa. 49:6)

And the light, as the Gospel tells us, shines from the cross,
on which the servant of the Lord was lifted up. The
eminent New Testament scholar Rudolf Bultmann
(1884–1976) states it well: "The request of the Greeks to
be led to the historical Jesus finds no fulfillment; it is a
false request. . . . *Through his passion* Jesus will become accessible for them as the exalted Lord." But there is one final point that remains to be added.

III

Our Gentile world beyond ancient Judea has access to
Jesus only through the witnesses of his glorification, who
proclaim Christ crucified to Jews and Greeks alike (1 Cor.
1:23–24). There can, of course, be no doubt that the "lifting up" of Jesus in our Gospel lesson means his crucifixion, which was also his glorification: the text tells us so
explicitly. But in his comments on an earlier passage in the
Fourth Gospel, John Calvin (1509–64) identifies the "lifting up" of Christ with preaching. John 3:14–15 reads:
"And just as Moses lifted up the serpent in the wilderness,
so must the Son of Man be lifted up, that whoever believes
in him may have eternal life." To be "lifted up," Calvin explains, means to be set in a prominent place, exposed to
everyone's view, and Christ is thus set before us in the
preaching of the gospel. He draws this conclusion: "No

one may complain of obscurity: this manifestation of Christ is open to all."

I will not vouch for Calvin's exegesis, but he has his theology right: the Son of Man, who was once lifted up on the cross, is lifted up again whenever the gospel is faithfully proclaimed and sealed by the sacrament of his body and blood. Those good souls who warn us of "bad news for believers" miss the point, which is that Christ is known to believers in the good news of the church's proclamation.

We don't seek Jesus in ancient history; the crucified and exalted Lord seeks *us* out in the company of the faithful and renews his claim on our lives. We can testify that he has done it before; whatever the latest results of the quest for the historical Jesus, we are sure he will do it again. We rightly call him "the Christ of faith," not as if our faith invented him, but because he is the one who has given us the gift of faith and constantly renews it as we gather to honor his name. And that, my fellow believers, is why we find it right and proper, after all, to say with the Letter to Timothy: "We are not ashamed, for we know the one in whom we have put our trust, and we are sure that he is able to guard until that day what has been entrusted to us."

The Living Word

*"You search the Scriptures, because you think
that in them you have eternal life;
and it is they that bear witness to me."*
John 5:39

With the beginning of Advent, Christians turn their thoughts to Bethlehem and the coming of the Savior into "this mortal life . . . in great humility." It is easy to see why one Sunday in Advent, the third, is set aside for John the Baptist, the messenger sent ahead by the Lord to prepare the way for his coming. Another, the second, serves as Bible Sunday, and why we link Advent with the Bible may not be so obvious. The passage of the Fourth Gospel from which my text is taken (John 5:39) gives us the reason: because John the Baptist and the Bible have for us exactly the same assignment, which is, to "prepare the way of the Lord"—to open up a plain, straight path for his advent into our lives.

Many of our churches are deeply troubled at the moment by the question, How should a Christian think of the Bible? I suppose one might say that they have been troubled for two hundred years. But the question peaks from time to time, and it has done so again in recent months. The Southern Baptists, for instance—who are among the strongest and most vigorous of our churches—have asked again whether their spiritual leaders still hold firmly to the strict inerrancy of the Bible.

The Presbyterians have been busy writing a new confession of faith. And I have been struck by the anxiety throughout the Presbyterian Church that the old loyalty to the Scriptures may be compromised. The committee entrusted with the task of drafting the new confession (of which I am a member) invited the counsel of others, both inside and outside the church. And again and again we were admonished: See to it that you reaffirm the old Reformed commitment to the Bible as the written Word of God!

It is tempting to take sides with one or another party on the points at issue. But not to preach a party sermon! The preacher's task is rather to bring to light the common ground on which we all stand, to remind the churches of what every Christian really knows already, and to help the rival parties to understand and trust one another. Not an easy assignment! But it's the only one I know.

There are at least three ways of looking at the Bible. They are different; but to take your stand on any one of them, you aren't required to call down fire from heaven on the other two. And I think it is clear that, within the Christian community, the third view—contained in my text—will immediately be recognized as saying the most important thing.

I

First, there are those who look at the Bible as *infallible words*—the "cover to cover" theory, if you like. In this view, the entire Bible, from Genesis to Revelation, consists of the lively oracles of God, given to the human authors by inspiration of the Holy Spirit. For, as the Bible itself attests, "all Scripture is inspired by God and is useful for teaching, for reproof, for correction, and for training in righteousness" (2 Tim. 3:16). Therefore, surely, no matter where you open your Bible and set your finger, it must fall on infallible words of God. "It is written" means "That is what God said."

The strength of this conviction will be clear to anyone who has ever listened to an old-style evangelist, every point introduced with an authoritative "The Bible says . . . " It may seem as if we have here a sure remedy for the primal sin, which was questioning the Word of God. The Fall began when the serpent, "more subtle than any other wild creature that the LORD God had made," asked: "*Did* God say . . . ?" (Gen. 3:1, RSV). The opening move was to sow doubts about the Word of God; then the serpent assured the woman that what God said was not so. What better remedy, then, than unquestioning acceptance of the words of God?

But others have felt that the cover-to-cover theory risks too much, for just one error in the Bible would seem to cast doubt over it all. This last summer, I had occasion to read the autobiography of an eighteenth-century skeptic who had been brought up on the strictest view of biblical authority. He tells how he came to question the truth of first one, then another biblical story. It is unbelievable, he says, that Joshua made the sun stand still at Gibeon (Josh. 10:13), or that the devil took Jesus to the holy city and set him on the pinnacle of the Temple (Matt. 4:5). "But if I rejected one [such story], then the credibility of them all collapsed, and with it the credibility of the Bible as divine revelation."

The champions of the cover-to-cover theory will reply that there are no proven errors in the Bible, only difficulties that can be explained. They may be right. But my skeptic was led to the second possible view of the Bible.

II

Like many other cultured despisers of popular religion, he came to look at the Bible simply as *literature*—a very remarkable collection of writings from bygone days, writings that the well-educated man or woman ought to know about. *The Bible Designed to Be Read as Literature* was the title of a book published in England and America some years ago (in 1936). The introduction made a case for Bible reading exactly parallel to the case for reading the Greek and Latin classics: We mustn't let our young people grow up ignorant of the foundations on which Western civilization is built. Such a voluntary starving of the mind, such unholy anorexia, would be incredible folly.

The second view, too, has its obvious merits, not least in a university setting like our own. The Bible was not revealed in solid, parallel columns, broken only by arbitrary divisions into chapters and verses. Nor does it all consist of straightforward information about divine things. It contains poetry, tales, proverbs, letters, and so on, none of which can be understood without regard for their special literary form.

And it is surely a great gain to read the Bible along with other literature, including other religious literature. The story has often been told of a meeting of the Free Religious Association of America, in Boston, at which a zealous minister recited passages from the Gospels and announced that they could not be matched in the sacred books of any other religion. Ralph Waldo Emerson (1803–82), who was seated in the audience, rose and said quietly: "The gentleman's remark only proves how narrowly he has read." Well, perhaps it also proved how deeply the gentleman was committed to his own faith. But there is a zeal for God that is not according to knowledge (Rom. 10:2). And Christians are not required to believe that God talks only to them.

Still, the second view has its limits, doesn't it? It always strikes the devout as missing the Bible's main concern, which, they will say, is not culture but salvation. And I agree. Being saved and being civilized aren't the same thing. You can have either one without the other. But why not both?

III

That there is a third possible view of the Bible, I take to be the lesson of my text: the Bible as *witness*—witness to Jesus as the Living Word of God to us, "that was with the Father and was revealed to us" (1 John 1:2). Jesus had made some astonishing claims for himself. "Anyone who does not honor the Son does not honor the Father who sent him" (John 5:23). His critics charged that in calling God his Father—*his* Father—he made himself God's equal (v. 18). And the question, reasonable enough, was: Who says so?

Jesus replies that if he were himself his only witness, no court of law would hear him. But it is the Father who bears witness to him. The evangelist may have taken this to refer to the story of Jesus' baptism, at which a voice was heard saying: "This is my Son, the Beloved" (Matt. 3:17).

But we are also given to understand that the Father's testimony comes in three ways: through the witness of John the Baptist, through the witness of Jesus' own works—and through the witness of Scripture. Perhaps we are to understand, too, from John 5:38, that there is a fourth witness: the word within, without which no outward testimony ever quite convinces.

"You search the Scriptures, because you think that in them you have eternal life; and it is they that bear witness to me" (RSV). The Scriptures—including now the New Testament along with the Old—point beyond themselves, as John the Baptist did; they point, as Jesus' works did, to Jesus himself as the Living Word. There is a gentle rebuke in Jesus' words "You search the Scriptures, because you think that in them you have eternal life." Not that we should not search the Scriptures, but that we should not expect life from mere study of the letter. "They bear witness to me." In so doing, they open up the way for his advent into our mortal life.

We have all heard the famous dictum of William Chillingworth (1602–44): "The Bible, I say, the Bible only is the religion of protestants!" How utterly misleading that is! The religion of Protestants is no different from the religion of Catholics: it is faith in Jesus Christ as God's Word to us. The Bible is not our religion. We read it, as Christians, because it makes straight the way of the Lord, his ever-new advent into our lives. We search its pages again and again because there we meet the Lord who fills our emptiness with the bread of life, who lightens our darkness, who breaks the oppressive silence with his words of grace, who stabs us awake with his uncompromising demands.

"These writings," says Erasmus (c. 1466–1536), "bring you the lively image of His holy mind and the speaking, healing, dying, rising Christ himself, and thus they render Him so fully present that you would see less if you gazed upon Him with your very eyes." A more perfect statement of Christ's advent in the written word would be hard to find. But John Calvin (1509–64) comes close.

In an elegant passage on what the Christian reader should look for in the Bible, Calvin, like Erasmus, insists that the Scriptures have a center, a focus, a goal: every word, even of the Law and the Prophets, draws and brings us to the figure of Jesus Christ. "Our minds ought to come to a halt at the point where we learn in Scripture to know Jesus Christ and him alone, so that we may be directly led by him to the Father who contains in himself all perfection."

Because he understood the Bible's use in this way, Calvin could sometimes point out what he took to be mistakes in the Bible—for example, incorrect references of the New Testament to the Old. Perhaps these "difficulties" could be explained. Perhaps they weren't there in the original manuscript. But to Calvin they just don't seem to have mattered, because he knew how to go straight to the heart of the matter.

I think Emil Brunner (1889–1966), too, a theologian of our own century, made the point effectively in a striking illustration, though it suffers a bit from the passage of time. Some of you may still remember the old 78 rpm records with the HMV (or Victor Records) label. They pictured an antique phonograph (or "gramophone," as we used to say in the old country) with a handle to wind it up and a large horn for a speaker. A white-haired dog with black ears, his head a little on one side, is listening to "his master's voice."

> Everyone [Brunner writes] has heard the trade slogan "His Master's Voice." If you buy a gramophone record, you are told that you will hear the Master Caruso. Is that true? Of course! But really his voice? Certainly! And yet—there are some noises made by the machine which are not the master's voice, but the scratching of the steel needle upon a hard disc.

And Brunner's point is that you don't listen to the incidental noises, but to the master's voice.

The Master says: "You search the Scriptures, because you think that in them you have eternal life. And you are right if you understand that it is they that bear witness to me." "The one who testifies to these things says, 'Surely I am coming soon'" (Rev. 22:20). Even so, Lord, come quickly!

The Preeminence of Christ

(The Transfiguration of the Lord)

*"And when they raised their eyes
they saw no one but Jesus."*
Matthew 17:8

After the amazing event that has just been reported, this may sound like an anticlimax. We call the event the "Transfiguration of the Lord." The first three Gospels all describe it in detail, though in slightly different words, and we may be surprised at first that the Fourth Gospel doesn't mention it at all. But, for John, the whole of Jesus' life was a continual veiling and unveiling of the Word made flesh. Matthew (17:1–9), Mark (9:2–8), and Luke (9:28–36) concentrate the unveiling of Christ's heavenly glory in a single dazzling moment, which stands out dramatically from the wider narrative. And then, the words of my text seem to conclude, everything went back to normal: the three disciples saw only the familiar figure of Jesus. Or do the words have another, deeper meaning?

I

We read that Jesus took Peter, James, and John—the inner circle of his followers—and led them up a high mountain. Luke implies it was night, and he tells us that Jesus' intention was to pray. While he was praying, his appearance changed: his face began to shine with a strange radiance, and even his clothes turned dazzling white—whiter, says Mark, than you could bleach them. As the tired disciples watched in astonishment, Moses and Elijah appeared and spoke with Jesus. Confused and fearful, Peter did his best to say something suitable to the occasion. But a cloud enveloped him, and a voice from the cloud interrupted him; and the disciples all collapsed in terror.

There are at least three marvels here: the transformation of Jesus, the appearance of Moses and Elijah, and the sound of the heavenly voice. It is not surprising that many historians pass over the story in silence, or that the commentators, who cannot ignore it, ask themselves what it was that really happened. Is the story pure fiction? The earliest Christians anticipated that hypothesis. The Second Letter of Peter, as we call it, is attributed to Simon Peter himself. In that case, it would be the chief witness of the Transfiguration who writes: "We did not follow cleverly devised myths when we made known to you the power and coming of our Lord Jesus Christ, but we had been eyewitnesses of his majesty. . . . We ourselves heard this voice come from heaven, while we were with him on the holy mountain" (2 Peter 1:16, 18).

Is it then a legend with a historical core? And can we perhaps surmise that what really happened was not so supernatural as unenlightened Christians once imagined? The radiance of the Transfiguration, some suggest, may have been the morning sunlight rising over the misty peaks of the hills. Or, as Evelyn Underhill (1875–1941) proposed, it was an instance of a common enough phenomenon observed elsewhere: the aura that transforms the faces of the saints at prayer.

More ingeniously, Sir Arthur Conan Doyle (1859–1930) argued that we have here biblical evidence of the spiritualism that so intrigued him: an apostolic séance. Peter, James, and John formed a psychic circle and materialized the Old Testament heroes Moses and Elijah. For the creator of the world's greatest detective, it was elementary.

I hope you will excuse me if I don't attempt to adjudicate between these fascinating theories. In Matthew's version, the Transfiguration is called a "vision" (v. 9). I'll settle for that, because what we want to know is not how it happened, but what it means. The answer is in the verse I have taken as my text, which is not at all an anticlimax but rather tells us the moral of the story. Jesus came over to the terrified disciples, touched them, and told them to get up. (John Calvin [1509–64] comments: "Nor is it only by his words that he comforts, but by touching also that he encourages them.") "And when they raised their eyes, they saw no one but Jesus" (NJB). Moses and Elijah have disappeared. Jesus stands alone. That's the point.

To borrow a phrase from the Apostle Paul (Col. 1:18, KJV), the Transfiguration is about the "preeminence" of Christ, who is lifted up above even the best that went before him. He is peerless, without equal. Three talked together: Jesus, Moses, and Elijah. But when the disciples look up, they have eyes for Jesus only.

II

Notice, first, that the preeminence of Christ does not mean rejection of the Law and the Prophets. We misunderstand the story if we imagine a contest between the old and the new. Recall Jesus' words in the Sermon on the Mount: "Do not think that I have come to abolish the law or the prophets; I have come not to abolish but to fulfill" (Matt. 5:17). The account of the Transfiguration presents Moses, Elijah, and Jesus conversing amicably.

Care is certainly taken to exhibit a parallel between Jesus and Moses, between the revelation of the gospel and the giving of the law. Moses too went up a mountain with his chosen three. A cloud settled on Mount Sinai too, and God called to Moses out of the cloud (Ex. 24:9, 12–18). Because he had been talking with God, the skin of Moses' face shone too (34:29), like the face of Jesus afterward. Clearly, we are to realize that on the mountain of transfiguration something takes place that is no less momentous than the giving of the commandments at Sinai. But there is no trace of conflict: the gospel is the fulfillment of the law.

Elijah, of course, stands for the prophets as Moses does for the law, and here also there is perfect harmony between the old and the new. But why Elijah? Perhaps because he stood near the beginning of the long line of Hebrew prophets; more likely, because Jewish tradition held that, before the Messiah came, Elijah would return first as his forerunner (cf. Matt. 17:10). Once again the point is clear: the messianic age is breaking in, and the glory of the Transfiguration is the fulfillment of the expectations long cherished by Israel. If Jesus is now to move into first place in the devotion of Peter and James and John, he does so because his story is the goal of an older story, the denouement of a much larger plot that the disciples knew so well. And yet, his destiny is not at all what most of his people expected of their messiah.

For notice, second, that the preeminence of Christ does not spare him from suffering and death, but leads him necessarily to a cross. What, we wonder, did Jesus talk about with Moses and Elijah? Matthew doesn't say. Neither does Mark. But Luke tells us they talked about his "departure," his "exit" (Luke 9:31)—the death he was to "fulfill" in Jerusalem. (We don't usually speak of "fulfilling" our death. The word reminds us again that everything is proceeding in accord with a divine plan, to which Jesus is freely giving his consent.) Not even Luke says how Moses and Elijah may have responded to this thought: that Jesus' vocation was to be fulfilled in his death. He simply points the narrative toward the Passion. The Transfiguration falls between Caesarea Philippi and Jerusalem.

Most readers agree that the turning point in the Gospel narrative comes when Jesus decides at Caesarea Philippi that his disciples are ready to answer the crucial question: "Who do you say that I am?" (Matt 16:15ff.). It is Peter who replies. "You are the Messiah, the Son of the living God" (v. 16). Everything in the Gospels seems to turn around this pivotal moment of Peter's confession, and he is rewarded with Jesus' blessing and Jesus' promise to build the church on this rock (vv. 17–18). But, almost immediately, the rock becomes a stumbling block (v. 23): Peter cannot endure the announcement that the Messiah, the Son of the living God, will undergo great suffering and be killed. This time, Jesus rebukes him—and with a surprising harshness. "Get behind me, Satan!" (v. 23). In all three of the Synoptic Gospels, the Transfiguration comes next.

What, then, is the point of the story in its narrative context in the life of Jesus? It shores up Peter's confession against the evil day that is coming. It identifies Jesus once again—reminds the disciples who he is—because the hour of his humiliation is near, and Peter's confession (already compromised) is going to be tested to the limit. For a brief moment, the veil is lifted, and the favored three disciples catch a glimpse of the glory of Christ in the humanity of Jesus. Surely such a demonstration of royal splendor will see them through their ordeal! But it doesn't. When the day arrives and the Lord is betrayed, arrested, and put on trial, Peter fails him: not trusting the vision that came to him on the mountaintop, he denies his Lord. Or is it possible that he never understood the vision?

For notice, lastly, that the preeminence of Christ summons his disciples to undivided loyalty whatever the cost (see Matt. 16:24). Peter misses the point. Seeing Jesus conversing with Moses and Elijah, he appears to be excited to find his master in such exalted company. According to Mark (9:5), he calls Jesus "Rabbi" and proposes to set up three "tabernacles" (KJV) to celebrate the meeting of three great teachers. And the voice from heaven says: "This is my Son . . . ; listen to him!" (Matt. 17:5). Moses and Elijah vanish. No one is left except Jesus.

Jerome (c. 347–c. 420) comments: "You are wrong, Peter. . . . Do not seek for three tabernacles. There is but one tabernacle of the gospel, in which the law and the prophets are to be recapitulated." The comment is sound. But more, surely, is intended. Here is no ordinary teacher, and he demands no ordinary loyalty. For all his great confession at Caesarea Philippi, Peter does not grasp the point.

III

And what does the Transfiguration mean to us now? Not presuming to ask what really happened, I have simply told the story from the standpoint of Peter and his friends, as you will have realized. But what does it say to us, who stand on the other side of Easter? The problem, according to Mark's editorial comment (9:10), is that the disciples didn't understand Jesus' talk about rising from the dead. The vision of Jesus transfigured was granted them as a foretaste of future glory, but it didn't see them through. Are things easier for us, then, who look back to the resurrection as the Lord's triumph over death? I doubt it.

When the clouds move in, we still have trouble remembering the vision on the mountaintop. It is a hard lesson to learn: that we should trust those rare moments of clear insight and heightened joy that are granted us from time to time, and should let them help us through the long hours of doubt and sadness. These other times will come; if you don't know it already, you can believe me. But when we can no longer see the hand of the Heavenly Father, we may still hear the voice: "This is my Son . . . ; listen to him!"

In one respect, I think, things may actually be harder for us these days. The world has grown larger, and we ask ourselves, How can we possibly reconcile our undivided loyalty to Christ with our awareness that there are, after all, many masters—that lots of people who are at least as wise and good as we are turn from him and place their trust in someone else? Is there a little presumption, along with our loyalty, when we say, "No one but Jesus"? Maybe there is. But I am not sure that there needs to be.

Some years ago, a good friend of mine who had been brought up in a strict Christian home wrote to tell me that she had converted to Judaism. "You will be shocked," she said. I really wasn't. You may think I should have been. But I knew that there were some things in Christianity that got in the way of her faith in God. I could not bring myself to admit that any of them could be blamed on Jesus! But I remembered how our New Testament professor at seminary told us repeatedly that the best interpreter of Jesus was a Jewish scholar, Claude Montefiore (1858–1938). I decided I didn't need to be shocked.

I wish it were not found necessary by some earnest Christians to see the devil at work whenever they run across a faith that is not the exact mirror image of their own. Like James and John in the Gospel, they seem eager to call down fire from heaven on anyone who will not receive the Lord. We can only ask them to remember that Jesus rebuked James and John, and led them on to the next village (Luke 9:52–56).

The Creator must love variety, since the world is so full of it. We are summoned to be loyal to the best we know, and to bear faithful witness to it. We are not required to deny that the eternal goodness we believe in may reach out to others in other ways. Indeed, we are forbidden to deny it if the tabernacle of the gospel somehow covers the law and the prophets. When Peter and James and John raised their eyes, they saw no one but Jesus. And yet, what they saw in him was the eternal goodness in which we live and move and have our being (see Acts 17:28), and which has never been without a witness (14:17). May we all see the Redeemer in the same way, with the same eyes!

For and Against

"Whoever is not against us is for us."
Mark 9:40

I can never read those words without recalling that they were once assigned to me, more than thirty years ago, as the text for a trial sermon. I was a seminary student at the time, and it was the president of the school himself who chose the text for me. He was a charming, gentle liberal, whose faith had none of the sharp edges mine then did. I may have imagined it, but I suspected then, and still do, that the text was meant to place a mild question mark over my passion for exposing heretics in the church. That was a very long time ago.

In any case, on receiving my text in a note from the president, I marched off to his lodge and reminded him that it is also written, in Matthew 12:30, "Whoever is not with me is against me." I had the impression I made him nervous. I could have imagined that, too. But he did what he always did when he wasn't quite sure what to say: he rolled a strip of paper between the palms of his hands while he gazed thoughtfully at his shoes, his head inclined slightly to one side. Finally, he looked up with a cheerful smile and gave me his reply: "Gerrish, my friend, you may preach on *both* texts."

Actually, that's what I wanted. And I still remember how I left him, confident that I had added my valiant amen to the litany of Bishop J. C. Ryle (1816–1900):

> From the liberality which says everybody is right,
> From the charity which forbids us to say that
>   anyone is wrong,

>   From the peace which is bought at the expense of
>   truth—
>   May the good Lord deliver us.

But what a heavy price I had to pay! I had committed myself to preach on two texts—one tailor-made for the elastic liberal, and one for the guardians of exclusive orthodoxy. "Whoever is not against us is for us." "Whoever is not for me, with me, is against me." The two texts plainly contradict each other. Or do they? Well, let's think about it. Perhaps it is significant that while Mark has the first saying, and Matthew the second, Luke found room for them both (9:49–50; 11:23).

I

The first saying, "Whoever is not against us is for us," was Jesus' comment on an incident reported to him by John, the son of Zebedee.

The disciples had seen a man casting out demons in Jesus' name; and because he did not follow them, they tried to stop him. More about this strange exorcist is not told us. It may even be that the name "Jesus" was nothing more to him than a magical formula that worked miracles. But if so, it doesn't seem to have been this that the disciples objected to. The problem, in their eyes, was simply that he wasn't one of them, and they were jealous for their rights and privileges.

You may remember that, as the story has come down to us, the disciples had just been debating that most momentous of all theological questions: Which of us is the greatest? They had rank, privilege, and exclusive rights on their minds.

As so often, the Savior's answer immediately changes the issue. "Do not stop him; for no one who does a deed of power in my name will be able soon afterward to speak evil of me" (v. 39). Of "me"! What matters is not the dignity of the disciples, but the honor of their Lord. The man may have been slighting what the disciples took to be their exclusive rights, but what does that matter? He was doing

Christ's work—and apparently with some success. Hence our first saying, "Whoever is not against us is for us."

Or, as a variant reading has it: "He that is not against you is for you. The one who is far off today will be close tomorrow." In other words: Rejoice at what this one achieves in the name of Jesus today, and tomorrow, perhaps, this person will be one of us. This individual may not be of our *circle;* but if we get our priorities right, we can surely see that he or she is on our *side.* The kingdom of heaven has enemies enough without trying to shut out tomorrow's friends.

The second saying, "Whoever is not with me is against me," was occasioned by the astonishing public response to Jesus' own success in casting out demons. A crowd gathered to watch, and they began to wonder: Can this be the Son of David? But Jesus' enemies were unimpressed: Yes, he casts out demons—they couldn't deny that—but he does it, they said, by the power of the prince of demons.

This time, Jesus' reply ends with a sharp warning. He sheds no light on the question why his enemies wished to deny his mission. Did they, too, like Jesus' disciples, want to protect their rights and privileges as God's sole agents in the world? Very likely. But we don't really know. Jesus simply warns them to consider what their opposition means.

Unless the kingdom of evil is divided against itself, he cannot be on the side of evil. "If [then] it is by the Spirit of God that I cast out demons, then the kingdom of God has come to you. . . . [And] whoever is not with me is against me" (vv. 28, 30). Once again, the issue is turned around. It is not a question of whose side Jesus is on. His critics had better be asking themselves whose side *they* are on. They cannot merely stand aside and scoff. There are no half measures; there is no sitting on the fence, no neutrality, no looking on. The kingdom of God has come! Even not to decide is to decide against it.

II

Now if you look at the commentaries, you will find that they all, without fail, refer you from either one of our two sayings to the other. Some tell you forthrightly that the sayings are contradictory; others, more cautiously, that they appear to be contradictory. But this is to overlook an important difference between them, which finally dawned on me those many years ago as I spent an anxious week struggling with my assigned texts. Maybe I looked at the wrong commentaries.

The difference, to put it in our own situation, is this: the first saying tells us how to think of the other person, while the second tells us how to think of ourselves. The first, "Whoever is not against us is for us," calls for generosity in our estimate of others; the second, "Whoever is not with me is against me," calls for honesty in testing ourselves. By the one, we accept the profession of others; by the other, we try our own profession. One says, "Judge not"; the other says, "Examine yourself."

It further dawned on me that if this crucial difference between the two sayings removes the apparent contradiction, there is also a crucial likeness between them that makes them both, in the end, say exactly the same thing. For both judgments—on the other and on ourselves—are to be made by one and the same standard, which is undivided commitment to Christ and his cause. The problem in both of our two Gospel stories is that something else was permitted to get in the way of this commitment.

Why was it, in particular, that the disciples wanted to stop that other man? Not, apparently, because they were greatly worried about his loyalty to their Master, but because he wasn't one of them. And if that is so, then was it *his* profession of Christ's name that was in question, or *theirs*?

John told the Master, perhaps expecting to be praised, that he and his friends had stopped the man from casting out demons in Jesus' name; and Jesus replied, "Whoever is not against us is for us." But he might just as well have said: John, are you really with me? Or is there something you value more than loyalty to me? Are you more concerned for your group than for my name? He said: "Whoever is not against us is for us." Might he not just as well have said, "John, whoever is not with me is against me"?

III

More than three decades have passed since the ordination requirements of my church forced me to wrestle with my two texts. In some ways, they have been gloomy decades. But they also span a period in the life of all the churches when the lesson of the texts has been marked as never before, whether or not the texts have been expressly quoted to teach the lesson. We are all, I think, much less quick than we used to be to inform the Lord that some of those who cast out demons in his name don't really belong, that they're not our kind.

In the life of the church, the "great new fact" of the twentieth century, as the church historians say, is the ecumenical movement, which has brought the separate churches together in a new sense of unity. And what are the conditions of this unity? It helps, no doubt, that we are more ready to acknowledge the possibility of error, even in our own church. To my spiritual forefathers, three centuries ago, Oliver Cromwell (1599–1658) addressed the entreaty: "I beseech you, in the bowels of Christ, think it possible you may be mistaken." Yes, it is possible! And we realize now that if a special mansion were reserved in heaven for all who claim to possess absolute truth, then one corner of heaven itself would be—well, more like the other place.

But it is not really the possibility of error that has made us grow together. It is the recognition that the Lordship of Christ transcends even our most sacred traditions; and that exclusiveness, if we persist in cherishing it, may place a question mark over our ultimate loyalty. Is it, after all, really to Christ and his cause that our commitment is given? Or do we cherish more the excellence of our own ecclesiastical pedigree, the perfection of our own creeds, the splendor of our own liturgies, and heaven knows what else—all, finally, because they are ours?

Grace, like genius, is bestowed without respect of persons, of race, or of denomination. Christ makes himself Lord over the lives of men and women with a sovereign disregard for which church they happen to attend. And the God who can raise up children unto Abraham from the very stones of the ground (Matt. 3:9) raises up our spiritual leaders in many corners of Christendom. We listen to them, not because they are ours, but because we believe they are God's: because we recognize in their fallible human accents the echo of Christ's own words.

As one of my favorite theologians (Friedrich Schleiermacher, 1768–1834) wrote more than a century and a half ago: "All who start from the living word of the Saviour, and from living faith in him, stand on the same ground with us; and there can never be a reason for us to withdraw from fellowship with them." It has taken Christians a very long time to learn that lesson. And perhaps now we can take a second look at our many traditions and ask, not "Which of us is right?" but, "Have *they* seen something in their encounter with the Lord which *we* have missed in ours, or not seen so clearly?"

I can still say with the psalmist, "The boundary lines have fallen for me in pleasant places;/I have a goodly heritage" (Ps. 16:6). But I can also say: "It is just as well that God, in God's manifold wisdom, did not make the whole world Presbyterian." And I trust that you can not only agree with me but say the same thing for your own "goodly heritage."

The kingdom of God has come—that's what really matters. And if we cannot now say, "Whoever is not against us is for us," we hinder its progress and must hear the Lord's other word: "Whoever is not with me is against me."

Christi the Kingmaker

(Festival of Christ the King)

*"To him who loves us and has freed us from our
sins by his blood, and has made us kings and
priests to his God and Father,
to him be glory and dominion for ever."*

Revelation 1:5–6

A splendid doxology, fit for the day when many of our
churches are celebrating the festival of "Christ the King"!
The language soars, as it ought to, and it may show poor
judgment on my part if I now turn a doxology into the text
for a plodding sermon. You would certainly not thank me
if I took you through all the laborious textual and linguis-
tic problems that the scholars find in this one brief sentence. Some things are better kept for the classroom. But
there is a remarkable feature of verse 6 that I do want to
comment on, since it may help us to pay due homage to
Christ the King. The doxology names him, in effect, not
King, but Kingmaker. It says: "[He] has made *us* kings and
priests."

I am giving the text after the version followed by Martin Luther (1483–1546) in his German Bible. You'll find
the same wording in the old King James Bible, though not
in the Revised Standard Version (or the New Revised
Standard Version). "[He] has made us kings and priests."
Quoted in this form, the text is one of the Scripture proofs
commonly cited for Luther's doctrine of the priesthood of
all believers, and many people will tell you that the priesthood of believers is what the Reformation was all about.
But in Luther's own mind that's only half a doctrine: the
other half, usually forgotten, is the kingship—and I trust

it is not amiss to add, the queenship—of all believers. In his little treatise *On Christian Freedom* (1520), Luther tells us that Christ himself is king and priest, by right of birth, and imparts both of these two prerogatives to anyone who believes in him. "Hence we are all priests and kings in Christ, as many as believe on Christ." John Calvin (1509–64) agrees: Christ, he says, was anointed not for himself only, but for his whole body; the anointing is "diffused" from the head to the members.

We have to leave the priesthood of believers for another day and look, for now, only at the other, neglected half of Luther's doctrine. Our kingship, he says, is a "spiritual dominion." Calvin again agrees. He writes (in his schoolmastering style): "I come now to kingship: it would be futile to talk of it without first admonishing my readers that its nature is spiritual."

Now I am not convinced that a spiritual dominion is all the book of Revelation meant when it spoke of the saints as "reign[ing] with Christ" (20:4; 22:5). Saint John the Divine may have had something quite earthy in mind. I'm not sure. (Luther himself once remarked, as I recall, that the book of Revelation needs a revelation to explain it.) But if we place our text alongside others that Luther and Calvin liked to quote, then I do believe their thoughts on a spiritual kingship capture an important biblical theme— otherwise, there would be no point in mentioning them. "[He] has made us kings." Taking our clues from other Scripture passages, let's ask three questions: What does it mean? Is it realistic? How does it happen?

I

On the first question: The point is that the Scriptures sometimes lead us to think of kingship—God's kingship, Christ's, and ours—as inward and spiritual. The contrast is with misconceptions that would make it something outward and tangible, to which we might point and say: This is it! Our present-day New Testament scholars aren't sure whether Jesus really said to the Pharisees, "The kingdom of God is *within* you," which is how Luther and Calvin understood Luke 17:21. (That's also how the verse is given in the King James Version.) Jesus may have meant, "The kingdom is *among* you"—in your midst, not in your hearts. But Calvin and Luther found the spiritual kingship in two other Scripture passages as well.

In John 18, Pilate interrogates the prisoner to see if he has political ambitions and dreams of overthrowing the Roman provincial government. Did Jesus claim to be a king? Jesus answers: "My kingdom is not from this world. If my kingdom were from this world, my followers would be fighting to keep me from being handed over" (v. 36). Pilate persists: "So you *are* a king?" Jesus replies that he was born "to testify to the truth" (v. 37). A royal birth, indeed! But not one that Pilate needs to worry about. For what is truth? (v. 38). And he "would not stay for an answer," as Francis Bacon (1561–1626) put it.

A quite different misconception appears in Romans 14. There we hear of Christians who were bitterly divided over the question of what a Christian is permitted to eat and drink. Those who kept strict rules of abstinence felt superior to those who didn't, and those who didn't were contemptuous of those who did. Paul's verdict favors neither party: the debate confuses faith with unimportant externals. "For the kingdom of God is not food and drink but righteousness and peace and joy in the Holy Spirit" (v. 17). For Paul, at any rate, the kingdom was within.

But, of course, it is not just a matter of ferreting out texts, but of forming a picture of a certain kind of person that meets us in the pages of the New Testament. Jesus before Pilate shows his spiritual dominion in his faithfulness to the royal mission for which he was born—in his refusal to be deflected by other people's expectations or opposition. And it is the same picture of inward and spiritual dominion that we see, sometimes, at least, in his followers, when they recognize that the kingdom of God is righteousness and peace and joy.

In one of my favorite Sydney Harris columns, he tells of a Quaker friend of his, who walked with him one evening to the newsstand, paid the surly vendor for a paper, and thanked him politely. The man said nothing, not even a word of acknowledgment. "A sullen fellow, isn't he?" Harris remarked. His friend shrugged his shoulders and said: "Oh, he's that way every night." "Then why do you continue being so polite to him?" The answer was: "Why should I let *him* decide how I'm going to act?"

"Why should I let *him* decide how I'm going to act?" That, it seems to me, at the most elemental level, is "spiritual dominion": a sovereign disposition that doesn't relinquish control over its own inner self. "My friend," Harris comments, "*acts* toward people; most of us *react* toward them."

II

But is it realistic (second question) to hope for spiritual dominion as we move down from the basic level of daily incivility to oppression and brutality? I suppose that none of us can know for sure the point at which we ourselves might lose the battle. We can only learn from history that there seems always to be the possibility of victory. And it isn't confined to believers in Christ.

Take, for instance, that remarkable sage of imperial Rome, Epictetus (c. 55–c. 135), who has so often been compared with Jesus and called "the friend of God." Born into slavery and crippled—perhaps by a brutal owner—his one passion was for freedom. But he learned that the friends of kings, and even the king of Persia, were not free to do as they chose. To get where they were, or to stay where they were, they enslaved themselves to the things they wanted to possess but could never make secure against misfortune. The only thing that is always in one's own power, Epictetus decided, is one's own self. For if I must be chained, must I also weep? Even in his last years, freed from slavery but a captive of pain and old age, Epictetus could still say: "What else can I, a lame old man, do but sing hymns to God?" He didn't say the last word about either oppression or pain. But he did achieve an inner sovereignty that was to make him, after his death, the object of admiration of the emperor himself (Marcus Aurelius, 121–180 C.E.).

In our own time, one of the most persuasive witnesses to spiritual dominion has been the psychiatrist Viktor Frankl (1905–97), who wrote a best-seller on his experiences in Auschwitz and Dachau (*Man's Search for Meaning*). "The best of us," he admits, "did not return." The survivors were mostly those who abandoned every principle in order to survive. But Frankl remembers those who walked through the huts comforting others, giving away their last piece of bread; and he remembers those who did not disappoint the living, but entered the gas chamber upright, saying the Lord's Prayer or the *Shema Yisrael*. And he finds in these rare spirits proof that the last human freedom cannot be taken away: the freedom to choose one's attitude under any circumstances.

Is it realistic to speak of an inward sovereignty under any circumstances whatever? For the church, the answer comes from the cross, where Christ the King is an object of ridicule wearing his crown of thorns. It is a mistake to think that only the resurrection turns his humiliation into victory, or that only his coming again in judgment will reveal his power and glory. The victory and the judgment are already there in the words "Father, forgive them" (Luke 23:34), and, "Father, into your hands I commend my spirit" (v. 46). And there, too, is the answer to my third question.

III

How does it happen that we ourselves are made kings and queens to God? It happens as we are drawn into the story of Christ the King and hear his word. It happens by faith. "This is the victory that conquers the world, our faith. Who is it that conquers the world but the one who believes that Jesus is the Son of God?" (1 John 5:4–5).

Some may insist that this is the only way it happens, or can happen, and they may think it disloyal to Christ the King to admit any other possibility. But what then becomes of Epictetus, the friend of God, or the Jewish martyrs of the Holocaust? I think it would be presumptuous of us not to learn from their stories. We are not required, as Christians, to close our eyes to the evidence that God is never left without a witness (Acts 14:17). But we do gather to pay homage to Christ our King and Kingmaker.

Others may prefer the agnostic defiance of Henley's "Invictus" (William Ernest; 1849–1903):

> I thank whatever gods may be
> For my unconquerable soul
> . . . .
> I am the master of my fate:
> I am the captain of my soul.

Henley, like Prometheus, shook a fist at the gods, and that too is something we can understand. But faith is not weakness, even if believers admit that they are glad not to find themselves wholly alone, with just the created good of their own free spirit. We come to give thanks for the superadded grace of our redemption.

It is Christ the King who makes us kings and queens by the transforming power of his word: "But I say to you, Love your enemies and pray for those who persecute you" (Matt. 5:44).

It is Christ the King who makes us kings and queens by the transforming power of his own victory; "I have said this to you, that in me you may have peace. In the world you have tribulation [Luther translates: "In the world you have *Angst*," anxiety.] But take courage; I have conquered the world" (John 16:33).

And now "to him who loves us and has freed us from our sins by his blood, and has made us kings and priests to his God and Father—to him be glory and dominion for ever."

Transformation

Sin

"Your brother's blood is crying
out to me from the ground."
Genesis 4:10

"How much more shall the blood
of Christ . . . purify your conscience
from dead works to serve the living God."
Hebrews 9:14

I ask you to picture, for a moment, the dining room of a
well-to-do suburban household somewhere in England. It
is evening, and a little party is in progress. The engage-
ment of the daughter has just been announced, and the
family is celebrating in company with the young future
son-in-law.

All are in the very gayest of spirits. The girl is marry-
ing somewhat above her class, so mother has no
complaints. Neither has the young intended, for his
bride-to-be is an extremely attractive woman. Father is
especially jubilant: business is good, and, what's more,
he's in the running for a knighthood in next year's honors
list. As for the son—well, any excuse for an extra glass of
port is welcome enough to him.

But then, with startling abruptness, the party is interrupted. A mysterious police inspector appears. A young
girl, he reports, has just died in the infirmary; she has
committed suicide by swallowing a strong disinfectant,
and has burned out her insides. Nasty business? Yes, but
what has it to do with our charming family? After all, they
couldn't be held responsible for some unknown girl's suicide. That was *her* affair, not theirs. It was really too bad

of the inspector to cast this cloud of gloom over their fes-
tivities. And then the truth comes out.

I

The girl had left a diary in her room. Her story began
in a factory. She was a good worker—one of the best. But
she led a deputation for a few pennies' raise in pay. She had
to go, of course. Her employer found her a nuisance: the
new rate would have meant a 12 percent increase in labor
costs. So she was fired. And that shrewd employer, it turns
out, is none other than the father in our little family.

The girl's parents were dead, and she had no home to
go to. She managed to find lodgings, but her pay at the
factory had been too poor for her to have saved much; labor was cheap, and work was hard to find. She was near to
starving by the time she found another job. By a stroke of
fortune—good fortune for her—an influenza epidemic
robbed a nearby milliner of half her staff, and so the girl
was taken on. Again she worked well, and again she was
fired—this time because a wealthy customer happened to
be in a sour mood and lost her temper. Of course, the girl
had to go. The customer may not always be right, but the
wealthy customer certainly is. And that wealthy customer
is the daughter in our little family.

Next, a handsome young knight came to the girl's rescue: he offered to find her an apartment and to pay her
rent. Down-and-out as she was, she couldn't very well
refuse, though her pride was deeply wounded. Then her
benefactor became her lover; but when he was tired of
her, he ditched her. That generous and handsome young
cavalier is the fiancé of the daughter in our little family.

And then our heroine was picked up by a harmless
young lad whose only weakness was that he drank too
much. The affair led to pregnancy. But when the wild
young fool offered the girl stolen money, she had the dignity to refuse it. He deserted her. And that harmless
young blade is the son in our little family.

In desperation the girl appealed to the Women's Charity Organization. But because her spirit was not quite bro-

ken—because, in fact, she made the mistake of sticking to the truth—the committee disbelieved her story, and their most prominent member, a highly respectable and irreproachable lady, lost patience with her. The appeal was turned down. And that highly respectable lady is, of course, the mother in our little family.

There was now nothing left at all for the wretched girl, soon to become a mother. What could she have done once her child was born? There was nothing left for her—except the disinfectant.

The story, as many of you will have recognized, comes from J. B. Priestley's (1894–1984) play *An Inspector Calls* (1946). You may not think it a very good play—too many coincidences! But it has a very good moral. I give it in Priestley's own words, put into the mouth of the inspector: "There are millions and millions and millions of Eva Smiths and John Smiths . . . with their lives, their hopes and fears, their suffering and chance of happiness, all intertwined with *our* lives, what we think and say and do. We are members of one body. We are responsible for each other."

II

Whatever Became of Sin? So Karl Menninger (1893–1990) asks in the title of one of his books. And, to our embarrassment, he directs the question, as a psychiatrist, to the Christian church and its clergy.

Well, one thing that happened to sin, as Menninger himself suggests, is that it got lost in "collective irresponsibility." He is thinking of those massive, monstrous injustices inflicted by one group on another: the enslavement of African Americans, the mass murder of Native Americans, the exploitation of labor, the horrors of Auschwitz and Buchenwald, the My Lai massacre, the pollution of our environment . . . and he would no doubt add today the wholesale destruction of the "boat people" and of thousands upon thousands of innocent Cambodians.

And who, he asks, is guilty of such atrocities? Not I. I only obeyed orders, or only passed them on. How can I, an individual, be held accountable for what was done by a group to which I just happened to belong, or perhaps did not obviously belong at all? Sin has become so personalized and individualized, that we have difficulty perceiving our own guilt in the wrongdoing of our race, our nation, our class, our corporation.

This is not far from what I have in mind as the moral of Priestley's play. But why limit "collective irresponsibility" to those visible, monumental, and occasional crimes against humanity—crimes that appall and sicken us by their sheer arithmetical magnitude, even if we don't feel the guilt of them in our own conscience? There is also a collective irresponsibility by which we shrug off our trivial, everyday lapses from grace as though they could not possibly matter. They really do matter, if only we can see ourselves not as isolated individuals, but as part of a bundle of humanity.

If the knife were put into my hand, I cannot conceive of any circumstances under which I would take another's life. And yet, if I would never rise up like Cain and slay my brother or sister with a single blow, I do in fact rise every morning with the power in my hands, along with others, to destroy a human life by inches. Together we may find ourselves party to a crime we would not dream of committing directly and on our own. We may ask God defiantly, as Cain did, "Am I my brother's keeper?" and not wait for an answer. But make no mistake about it: the voice of our brother's blood cries out to God just as the blood of Abel did.

"We are responsible for each other." What killed Eva Smith, the girl in Priestley's play? Was it disinfectant self-administered? Or was it the one-track mind of a sharp businessman? Was it the momentary lapse in temper of a very proper young lady? Was it the very human frailty of a nice, but weak-willed young man? Was it the few "wild oats" of a not uncommonly hotheaded youngster? Was it even the shocked indignation of a respectable woman, devoted to good works? Big business, bad temper, fickleness, wildness, smugness—these are the things that together took Eva's life from her before she surrendered it herself.

Sin is collective irresponsibility, or shall we now say "cumulative guilt"? The sin I am talking about is in fact, as you may have noticed, "original sin." It is the sin that rises from the fact that we simply are *not* little islands separated by the sea, but one great landmass of humanity. Our lives are so bound up with one another that we share even in one another's guilt: not even our sins are our private concern, because they have a grim habit of ensnaring other people in their meshes.

The theologian Emil Brunner (1889–1966) somewhere offers a striking simile of this mysterious oneness of all humanity in sin. He says we are "like the individual strawberry plants which, underneath the surface, are tied up with one another in a texture of roots." I think he is probably right in arguing that this is the real meaning of the biblical doctrine of original sin, namely, that all humanity is one whole, one lump, one "Adam" in sin.

And if this is the real meaning of original sin, then the entire popular misconception of it is turned upside down: it does not mean that *we* suffer for *Adam's* sin, but that *others* must suffer for *our* sins. Perhaps you know how Robert Burns (1759–96) parodied this much-misunderstood doctrine in "Holy Willie's Prayer," as though it taught that we all

> deserve [such] just damnation
>> For broken laws.
> Five thousand years 'fore [our] creation,
>> Through Adam's cause.

Well, that's not what original sin means. It means that we are all tangled up together in sin; and that means that God holds us guilty, not because *we* have fallen through *Adam's* sin, but because *our* sins have caused *others* to fall. Perhaps that's not exactly what the Apostle Paul meant (in Romans 5), but it may be the best we can do today with an idea that is powerful enough to stand a little development. And if this is the direction we are to take, then even the fearful verdict of Augustine (354–430) that humanity is a "mass of perdition" begins to make some sense.

It is, I think, only as we begin to understand how

closely our lives are intertwined with the lives of others, and how easily our lapses can ensnare them, that we shall recognize what a frightening power sin is. Father, in Priestley's play, denies any responsibility for the girl's suicide; after all, just dismissing her from her job couldn't really be considered the cause of her death.

INSPECTOR: What happened to her then may have determined what happened to her afterwards, and what happened to her afterwards may have driven her to suicide.

FATHER: Oh well—put like that, there's something in what you say. Still, I can't accept any responsibility. If we were all responsible for everything that happened to everybody we'd had anything to do with, it would be very awkward, wouldn't it?

INSPECTOR: *Very* awkward.

III

There is another story that points up the same frightening moral in a still more forceful way, because it is something more to us than fiction. I asked, "What killed Eva Smith?" Let me ask another question: "What killed Jesus Christ? Why did *he* have to die?"

Surely we miss the point of the story that leads from the manger to the cross if we see it from the start as a monstrous act of deicide, planned and executed by satanically evil murderers. The Pharisees and the Saducees, Judas and Peter, Caiaphas and Pilate, and all the others who in various ways contributed to the destiny of Jesus do not seem to have been notoriously wicked; and yet, between them, they wove a net of sin around him and brought him to the cross.

Perhaps we shall never know their motives for sure. But can we not say that the record as we have it tells as much about the frailty and pettiness of human nature as it does about demonic evil? The Pharisees were devout men but rigid, and they could not understand Jesus. Judas' betrayal and Peter's denial are acts of weakness more than of malice. And the Sadducees and Pilate seem to have offered Jesus simply as the sacrificial lamb on the altar of peace and prosperity. And so we might go on. And is it not just here that we find the deepest reason to say with the Apostle Paul: "Christ died for *our* sins in accordance with the Scriptures" (1 Cor. 15:3)?

Of course, there's more! The second story, the story of Jesus, does not end, like the story of Eva Smith, with its disclosure of our kind of sin. His death is not only judgment but grace; and the blood of Jesus, as the Letter to the Hebrews tells us, "speaks a better word than the blood of Abel," or, as the old King James Version has it, speaks "better things" (12:24).

Just how that happens is, for us today, hidden rather than revealed in the strange language of the sacrificial cult. But may we not at least say this much: that the grace of the Savior must surely draw us to itself in much the same way as our sin reaches him, through that same network of roots that makes us one with him (cf. Rom. 5:19)? Indeed, the inspector's words, "We are members of one body," take on a still deeper significance when we turn from sin to grace and ask how, as believers, we are related to Christ and his church.

And if in this life, because we are never free from sin, the blood of our brothers and sisters still cries out against us in condemnation, how much more shall the blood of Christ purify our conscience from dead works to serve the living God!

Fitting God In

"What are you doing here, Elijah?"
1 Kings 19:13

"How do you fit *God* in?" The question was put to me by a young researcher in behavioral science, someone for whom I have a special regard and affection. "How do you fit God in?" She didn't mean: How can anyone possibly make room for God, too, in an already crowded schedule? That would be a fair enough question, given the breathless pace at which we have to meet the demands of all our various roles in life—as students and teachers, homeowners and breadwinners, fathers and mothers, Democrats and Republicans, and whatever else. There is always something more to do first, before we can take time out for meditation. And however important we say our religion is to us, it is one of the easiest things to put off till tomorrow. How to make time for it is a good question. But it's not what my questioner was asking.

Hers was not Martha's problem in the Gospel—being too busy to sit for a while at her Lord's feet (Luke 10:38–40)—though I am sure that, like everyone else, she had more than enough to do. Rather, as a budding young scientist, she was fascinated by the problem the French astronomer Pierre-Simon Laplace (1749–1827) voiced so bluntly in his famous answer to the great Napoleon. Asked what he thought about God, he replied: "We have no need of that hypothesis." Why, indeed, do we churchgoers still talk about God, now that we can safely leave it to science to explain the way the world goes without mentioning God? How do we fit God in?

On another occasion, my favorite questioner had proposed to me the thesis that actually religion survives only as a crutch for the weak: healthy, self-reliant people will have no use for it. Weak and immature is no doubt how many of our critics think of us. Religion, they say, has become a vestigial appendix to human existence in the modern world. It's not that they haven't time for it: they have no need of its support, any more than Laplace needed God to explain how the universe works. They think they have outgrown religion.

I must add that, with her question and her thesis, my questioner did not sound so much hostile as intrigued. Well, perhaps there was a little bit of mischief in her eye, too, as happens when scientists talk to theologians. But she was a "preacher's kid" (as we say), who had never exactly rebelled against the church. I think she was honestly wondering if there was a way back. She told me that "Where does God fit in?" was the theme of a conference at her university, organized by scientists who were willing to take another look at the discarded crutches of religion. "How do *you* fit God in?" was addressed to me as a theologian who, despite the handicap of a classical education, might have some understanding for a scientist's point of view.

Now I could not hope to reach for my Bible and open it at the precise text at which the question is directly answered. We shouldn't expect the Bible to anticipate, and settle in advance, all the problems of the twentieth century—not, at least, in quite the way we put them. But it did occur to me later (which is when good answers usually come to me) that there is something pertinent to be learned from the old story of Elijah, which we read in part as our Old Testament lesson. We might well say that the story is about the disappearance of God from nature, and what happens next. If I were to take a particular verse as my text, it would be 1 Kings 19:13 (the question at the end): "What are you doing here, Elijah?" The answer to the question where God fits in is the counterquestion, Where do *you* fit in? If we can grasp the counterquestion as the "word of the Lord" (which is what it is called in verse 9), then we have our answer to the original question.

I

The contest on Mount Carmel between Elijah and the prophets of Baal, you remember, is one of the most amazing stories in the Hebrew Scriptures (1 Kings 18:17–40). It makes for a racy, even humorous narrative, in which the prophet of the Lord makes fun of pagan religion. The prophets of Baal call on their God in vain to light their sacrifice. They dance; they slash their frenzied bodies with knives. And Elijah taunts them, advising them to shout louder: perhaps their god is deep in thought, or has wandered out of hearing, or has fallen asleep. "But there was no voice, no answer, and no response" (v. 29).

As soon as Elijah calls on the Lord, his sacrifice is consumed by fire. He seals his victory by slaughtering the 450 rival prophets. (That's a part of the story we would happily ignore, but there it is.) And the final proof that the Lord is God comes when the drought is ended and heavy rain begins to fall (vv. 41–46). Here, plainly, the true God is made known in a spectacular display of control over the forces of nature.

But the display of divine power fails to win the people and their leaders. In the following chapter we find Elijah totally let down after his victory and wishing to die. A very human reaction to success turned sour, and it is portrayed with great psychological insight. The irony is that now it is *Elijah's* God who is voiceless and absent. On Mount Horeb (Sinai) he waits for a God who does not appear. First there is a violent wind; but the Lord is not in the wind. Then an earthquake; but the Lord is not in the earthquake. Then a fire; but the Lord is not in the fire. We are not told how the fury of nature may have affected the prophet, only the simple, painful fact that his God was not there.

What follows is known to us all from the famous words of the King James Version: "and after the fire a still small voice" (19:12). That may be close to the meaning of the Hebrew—another version has "the sound of a light whisper." And that is dramatic and fitting enough: after the boisterous din of nature's best show, a soft whisper. But

the New Revised Standard Version has the yet more
telling phrase: "after the fire a sound of sheer silence"—
an eerie silence of the sort you can (in a way) hear and feel.
But the silence is broken: the whisper becomes a voice,
and the voice becomes a question: "What are you doing
here, Elijah?" Finally, the prophet is sent on his way with
instructions from the God who was not in the wind, the
earthquake, or the fire. The silence is broken with a question—and a command.

As always, you will find readers who think they can tell
you what really happened to Elijah—at least on Mount
Carmel. They say there was a petroleum deposit in the
area; it was a highly volatile liquid, not water (as the people imagined), that Elijah gave them to pour on and
around his offering. He then used a piece of glass to ignite
the fuel with the rays of the sun. By all means believe it, if
it helps you. You may even believe, if you wish, that we
have here a singular triumph of early natural science, and
you may be willing to forgive the prophet for a little de-
ception in a good cause. But we will still want to ask if the
story tells us something about the human condition.

II

What can we learn from Elijah's fascinating encounter
with the absence and presence of God on Mount Horeb?

We can learn, first, that there is indeed an absence of
God from nature, or rather *a hiddenness of God in nature.*
For Elijah, God just wasn't there any more in the awesome exhibition of nature's power—even though it was
precisely such a display earlier that had vindicated his
faith. The Lord was not literally absent, like Baal on a
journey abroad, but for Elijah he was hidden. And we
must surely add that, for ourselves, God is twice hidden
when the wind, the quake, and the fire destroy human life,
limbs, and property. If we try too hard to discern the hand
of God in every natural disaster, we run the risk of falling
into the dismal "wisdom" of Ben Sira, who wrote that
"there are winds created for vengeance," that "fire and
hail and famine and pestilence, all these have been created

for [divine] vengeance" (Sir. [Ecclus.] 39:28–29). Christians don't have to believe that; it's a hypothesis we really don't need. We can leave it to the natural scientists to explain why this earthquake, or that famine, happened when it did.

I don't mean to say that nature is always and totally silent. Our scientists themselves don't require us to say that. Time and again they tell us how the way the whole intricate system of nature fits together can evoke a sense of awe that, for some at least, is a hairbreadth from belief in God. It remains as true as ever that "the heavens are telling the glory of God,/and the firmament proclaims his handiwork" (Ps. 19:1). But if we put it like that, it is not a matter of struggling to fit God into nature, but rather of asking where nature and we ourselves might fit into some larger purpose. Which brings me to the second point.

We can learn from Elijah's story that *there is a presence of God in God's Word to us.* The silence is broken by a gentle whisper that becomes a persistent question: "What are you doing here?" (This is the second time the question was put to Elijah in this self-same passage [vv. 9, 13].) The words echo the first recorded theological question, when the Lord God called to Adam in the garden and asked: "Where are you?" (Gen. 3:9). (Well, maybe that comes second, if you count the serpent's asking Eve whether God had really spoken [3:1].) "Where are you?" and "What are you doing here?" are not requests for information on the part of someone who doesn't know the answers: they are invitations to take stock of ourselves, much like the admonition of Socrates (c. 470–399 B.C.E.) that the unexamined life is not worth living. Our questions about God, if asked in sincerity, become questions about ourselves. We ask how to fit God into our world, and are asked in turn how we see ourselves fitting into the only world there is. The questioner is questioned. But it's no game. The counterquestion is the first step to answering the question we asked first.

One of the ways we get lost in the garden is, I think, by single-minded pursuit of our own field of inquiry, which we take to be all there is. It is so easy to imagine that our domain without a visible God, which we can make secure with our elegant formulas, is the real world. In 1992 we remembered the first controlled nuclear chain-reaction, carried out on the campus of the University of Chicago. One of the many scientists who visited Fermilab for the occasion remarked with understandable satisfaction: "Physics is a brand of science that tries to explain *reality* and how the *real* world works."

A fragment of the real world, certainly. But not the whole of it. There are less controllable human reactions that have at least as much to do with the real world that we have to live in day by day. We all recognize this as soon as the moral ambiguity of the atomic age itself strikes home, demanding moral choices of us that we must act on if the real world is to remain the habitable world. We don't simply observe the physical world; it is the stage on which we are summoned to act. That is why the voice bids us think again about where we are and what we are doing here.

In the third place, then, we can learn from Elijah's story that *the Word of God always comes to us as a claim, as a demand on our lives.* In the end, it is the command of God that tells us what we most need to understand about the world and our place in it. The God who is hidden in the turbulence of nature speaks unmistakably when it dawns on us that we cannot remain spectators in the balcony, but must become actors on the stage. "The commandment of the LORD is clear," says the psalmist, "enlightening the eyes" (Ps. 19:8).

"Clear"? Is it really clear? Yes, I think so—once we have heard it. And it really does open our eyes to see the world in a quite new way. But it can hardly be denied that we aren't always listening for it, and don't always see by its light. Sometimes a crisis jolts us out of our complacency and forgetfulness—as when we read that literally millions of our brothers and sisters are likely to starve to death unless they receive massive aid from the richly blessed. The still, small voice can "speak through the earthquake, wind, and fire" (as the hymn has it). You don't argue with it, but only ask: What can we do?

The church, if I dare so put it, is there to keep us listening between the crises. Again and again, skeptical friends assure me we don't need the church anymore, and it's hard to argue with them as long as the prophets of religion still want to slaughter one another by hundreds. Morality on crutches doesn't seem to be what it's really all about: humanity in a coffin is more like it. I can only say that there may yet be seven thousand who haven't bowed the knee to Baal (1 Kings 19:18). For them, at least, the church is not a crutch exactly; it's more like a hearing aid, to amplify the still small voice.

How do we fit God in? We don't. We simply acknowledge that "in him we live and move and have our being" (Acts 17:28). When God's ever-present Word seems faint, we turn to the still small voice made flesh in Jesus Christ. Of him it is written: "He will not wrangle or cry aloud, nor will anyone hear his voice in the streets." But he will "bring justice to victory" (Matt. 12:19–20). Listen to *him*.

Grace Demanding

"Blessed are those who walk
not in the counsel of the wicked,
nor stand in the way of sinners,
nor sit in the seat of scoffers."

Psalm 1:1

"Blessed [are those] whose transgression
is forgiven, whose sin is covered."

Psalm 32:1

Even if the only psalm you memorized in Sunday school was Psalm 23, you will surely recognize the stately cadences of the very first verse in our Psalter. It tells us of the company the righteous will never keep—not walking, not standing, not sitting. Their true companion, day and night, is the law of the Lord. They are the ones who are pronounced happy, while those they shun are destined to perish.

But if you turn the pages of your Psalter until you come to Psalm 32, you will find that happiness is given equally to just the opposite kind of people: "Blessed are those whose transgression is forgiven, whose sin is covered." Is there happiness, after all, also for those who cannot claim the blessing of Psalm 1—who have gone along with the wicked, dallied with sinners, drawn up an easy chair among the cynics? Indeed there is! And it could well be one and the same person who is declared "blessed" (or "happy") by both our psalms. Can you not even say, with perfect truthfulness, that the entire existence of every child of God moves between these two blessings, the blessing of innocence and the blessing of forgiveness?

I

I suppose that these days talk of the "righteous," who bury themselves in the law of the Lord, doesn't conjure up the most appealing of images. (Why is it that in the movies Bible readers usually turn out to be grim fanatics, who bring misery into other people's lives?)

When I first began to study the liturgy as a seminary student, I learned that John Calvin (1509–64) placed the reading of the Decalogue, which he put into French rhyme for the purpose, near the beginning of his Strasbourg rite. Each of the commandments was followed dutifully by the congregation's *Kyrie eleison* ("Lord have mercy"). In the first flush of evangelical fervor that had carried me to seminary, I found this piece of historical intelligence utterly mortifying. Lord have mercy, indeed! To the redeemed people of God, assembled to praise their Lord, could anything be more depressing? I was relieved to learn further that the Genevan authorities required Calvin to simplify his service of worship, and the Ten Commandments dropped out.

Over the years, I should like to think I have grown not cooler but wiser. I read Calvin's explanation of his liturgy and began to see its point. The confession of our sins and the reading of the Commandments, so it turned out, were but transient moments in a liturgical movement that attains its high point in praise and thanksgiving. The somber beginning leads on to the recognition that "as Jesus Christ has righteousness and life in himself . . . we are justified in him and live in the new life through the same Jesus Christ." The liturgy therefore moves us on to ask for the kindling of this life in ourselves. And from petition we turn, last of all, to intercession: for "the life of Christ consists in this, to seek and to save that which is lost."

That's not so bad, after all—although I do sometimes have the feeling that Calvin *liked* confessing his sins.

More important, I now ask myself: Is there anything our lawless society and our lawless selves more desperately need to hear than the stern, uncompromising "You shall not" of the Ten Commandments? Maybe reading the law Sunday after Sunday could become a bit depressing, but, for sure, it could not be half so depressing as reading the Sunday news. That's a devotional exercise that leaves one longing to know that somewhere there may be shepherds of the people who can ascend the hill of the Lord with clean hands and pure hearts, "who do not lift up their souls to what is false,/and do not swear deceitfully." For "they," says the psalmist, "will receive blessing from the LORD" (Ps. 24:3–5).

The law of the Lord, rightly understood, is not oppressive but reassuring: it is a covenant mercy, pure grace. You would not consider it anything but indifference, or weakness, or blindness if there were no point at which earthly parents would lay down the law to their children. Why, then, should we not find it reassuring that our God, like a good father or mother, does not leave us to our own devices but, when we turn to the right hand or to the left, lets us hear the voice behind us say, "This is the way; walk in it" (Isa. 30:21)?

But you don't hear the voice if your ear isn't practiced to listen. Take a little time to meditate with the psalmist. Swallow the scroll; and, like Ezekiel's "son of man," you may find it—to your surprise—sweet as honey in your mouth (Ezek. 3:3).

How well the psalmists understood all of this! They received the precepts of the Lord thankfully, as more precious than gold and sweeter than the honeycomb (Ps. 19:10). With a little bit of charity, we can even understand those remarkable psalms in which the author boldly stands before the Lord and professes his own righteousness. There is, I think, a quite innocent gladness that can claim: "I did not follow the herd. My hands are clean. I am thankful I did what I knew to be right, and I am ready to take the consequences." A man or woman of integrity perhaps has the right to know it.

Yes, but what a fearful temptation is there! Even the Pharisee in Jesus' parable thanked God for his merits; but it was the tax collector, who could not lift up his eyes to heaven, who went home justified (Luke 18:9–14).

A faithful member of C. H. Spurgeon's congregation assured him one day that she had not committed any sin for several weeks. "You must be very proud," he said. "I am," she replied.

II

"Blessed [are those] whose transgression is forgiven." Even the man or woman of integrity slips, and there remains nothing for it but to move from Psalm 1 to Psalm 32 and to implore the Lord to forget the transgression and remember the covenant. Of course, God does not literally "forget" our sins, as though they had never been. In sober truth, your past is always there, sin and all, making you what you are today.

What is strictly true—and it must be this we are asking for when we petition God not to remember our trespasses—is that past wrong can always be vanquished by the present good of another, who bears our sins and overcomes them. Forgiveness is the unexpected infusion of grace—not into our souls but into our situation, transforming it into something utterly new. And that is exactly what Christians confess as the meaning of the incarnation: the appearance of the Redeemer, through whom the blessing of forgiveness reaches us.

Now, as we read the story of Jesus must we not say that Psalm 32 proclaims, not just another blessing, but the greater blessing? From a dozen Gospel passages to which we might have turned, I chose the story of the elder brother—the part of the parable of the prodigal son that is often left out. Why, I wonder, don't we call it what it is: the parable of the two sons? Well, maybe because we have another parable with that title (Matt. 21:28–32). I don't know. Perhaps we could call it the "parable of the two brothers." What is its meaning for us?

Well, if God in heaven makes the sun rise on the evil and on the good and sends rain on the just and on the unjust, we dare not infer from our parable that God loves the prodigal more than the elder brother. But can it be doubted that the prodigal plumbed the depths of divine love more than his brother ever did—and therefore knew better what it means to be "sons of [our] Father who is in heaven" (Matt. 5:45, RSV)?

O felix culpa! Blessed fault of Adam: not because evil is good, but because God ordains humanity's sin for the sake of the greater blessedness. Rather a prodigal come home than a dutiful older brother who never left home, but never rejoiced in his father's presence. The blessing of the gospel is this: that, through forgiveness, the fallen are brought closer to God than they were before they left God.

It has been said that there are two sorts of Christian, the melancholy and the easygoing, and that it is the former who write books of theology; they hold a gun in the faces of their more cheerful brothers and sisters, to persuade them that their happy dispositions are nothing but the obstinacy of sin. A clever remark! But on behalf of the theologians I must insist that it is quite mistaken.

It totally misses the third sort of Christian—the sort the New Testament is most interested in—whose cheerfulness has been wrested by grace out of melancholy. It misses the fact that Christian rejoicing is joy over the wanderer come home. What moves the church to music and dancing is not the inborn sweetness of our happy dispositions, but the "triumph of grace" over our mistake in leaving home.

III

There is one more word that needs to be spoken. If we find ourselves driven by painful experience from Psalm 1 to Psalm 32, are we not also driven back again to Psalm 1? Forgiveness does not do away with the law but provides the deepest reason for keeping it. The third part of piety (after the knowledge of our misery and our redemption) is thankfulness; so the Heidelberg Catechism (1563) tells us, and then it proceeds—under the heading of thankfulness—to expound the Ten Commandments.

"The one to whom little is forgiven, loves little" (Luke 7:47).

"Go . . . do not sin again" (John 8:11). Why not? Because next time God may get you? No, sin no more because you are forgiven.

Nothing, it seems, demands so much of me as grace abounding. The law tells me to do this and that: grace claims me absolutely, telling me to repent. This is the profound insight that broke in on the hymn writer Isaac Watts (1674–1748) as he "surveyed the wondrous cross": love demands *all* ("my soul, my life, my all").

It is always possible to misunderstand law, to presume that its demand is met by expanding the Ten Commandments into 613. But in truth everything is said already in the preamble to the law: "I am the Lord your God, who brought you out of . . . slavery" (Ex. 20:2). The sum of the law is the answering love of the redeemed (Mark 12:30–31; cf. Deut; 6:5, Lev. 19:18). The language of law acquires its full significance only as it passes over into the language of love, and grace abounding becomes grace demanding.

It is a difficult art, we are told, rightly to distinguish law from gospel: what God demands of us from what God gives to us. And how profoundly true that is! The reformation of the church once depended upon it, and perhaps always does. Where the gospel's word of free, unconditional, sovereign grace is not distinctly heard, there is no church of Christ.

But a still more difficult art is to put law and gospel back together again, once they have been rightly divided. When you have mastered the more difficult art, you should be able to say two things: Thanks be to God for the gracious, saving gift of the law—and thanks be to God for the total demand of the unconditioned gospel.

Blessed indeed is the man or woman of integrity, whom the law of God has kept innocent. But still more to be blessed is the one who turns back to the commandments in love as a forgiven sinner, who has heard the patient Father behind the stern "No!" of the commandments.

Response

The Unquenchable Flame

*"This is the judgment, that the light has
come into the world, and people loved
darkness rather than light."*
John 3:19

The last judgment and the unquenchable flames of hell
were once favorite themes for Christian instruction. Not
that the teachers and preachers of the church were ever of
one mind when they spoke of heaven and hell. Some, for
instance, harbored the appalling hope that among the joys
of heaven would be a clear view of the lost souls in hell below. Others, softer-hearted, believed that as long as there
remained even one lost soul in hell, there could be no rest
in heaven.

In our own day, however, we no longer hear much either way about heaven and hell. Times have changed, and
you may not recall when you last heard a sermon on hell.
Peter Berger, it is true, has reminded us that some human
deeds are so monstrously evil that they seem to demand
"not only condemnation, but *damnation* in the full religious meaning of the word." He says: "Deeds that cry out
to heaven also cry out for hell." But mostly, we have left
hell to the popular evangelists, and we count ourselves too
sophisticated to believe in red devils and their steaming
cauldrons.

Yet, even when we have decided that the unquenchable
flames are not to be taken literally, there remains a great
deal about judgment in our Scriptures. It should not go
unheeded. It still demands our attention. What are we to
make of it? I suspect that enough of the old, literal hell
lingers on in our childhood memories so that thoughts
unworthy of God's character may enter our minds and
trouble our faith. If we turn to our New Testaments, we

may be surprised by what we find there on the theme of judgment. It is written of Christ that he came not to judge, but to seek and to save the lost (John 12:47; Luke 19:10). His story is a story of judgment withheld. The gospel reassures us that God is always pure love, and that only our unbelief can change God's love into an unintended judgment.

There are, then, three things that we have to think about: judgment unheeded, or the decline of belief in hell; judgment withheld, since Christ judged no one, as had been expected, but came only to save; and judgment unintended, because we judge ourselves, without meaning to, by what we make of God's love in Christ.

I

Consider first the decline of belief in hell—*judgment unheeded.* In some ways, this is a mark of progress. The elaborate portrayal of demons with pitchforks casting sinners into the unquenchable flames goes back to a time when few could read and pictures were among the church's most effective methods of instruction. Sometimes the images even had a touch of humor to them, since medieval men and women had a surprising ability to chuckle at the antics of devils even while taking them seriously. But the impression on the mind of a child could be devastating. And in time it became harder even for adults to separate out the core of truth in the pictures.

C. S. Lewis made the point effectively in the first chapter of his delightful book *The Pilgrim's Regress.* Young John, born in Puritania, is dressed up and taken to see the "Steward" (that is, the local minister). His parents go into the Steward's room first, and when they come out again, they are looking very grim, as if they've just been given bad news by the doctor. To John's surprise, as he takes his turn and enters the room, he is met by "an old man with a red, round face who was very kind and full of jokes." The conversation turns to fishing tackle and bicycles, and John's fears are quite forgotten.

But then, suddenly, the kindly old man takes down

from the wall a terrifying mask, claps it over his face, and tells John about the Landlord—who is very, very kind and, if John doesn't keep all the rules, will send him forever to a black hole full of snakes and scorpions.

The talk ends with the Steward repeating that the Landlord is "quite extraordinarily kind and good to his tenants, and would certainly torture most of them to death the moment he had the slightest pretext." But as John and his parents are leaving, the Steward bends down and whispers in his ear: "I shouldn't bother about it all too much if I were you."

The problem of a worn-out religious belief could hardly be put across more tellingly. The black hole remains only as an instrument to frighten a child into conformity. And the result is that the child has no peace day or night "for thinking of the rules and the black hole full of snakes." It is surely no great loss if we have come to recognize, these days, that more harm than good is done by filling a young child's mind with thoughts of physical torment.

Indeed, that young minds cannot handle thoughts of devils and the flames of hell is not so modern an insight as we imagine. John Calvin (1509–64), who said time and time again that the flames of hell are not to be taken literally, didn't include hell in his Geneva Catechism. He found no mention of it in the Apostles' Creed, and thought it best left out of the catechism. He has the minister ask: "Why . . . is there mention [in the Creed] only of eternal life and not of hell?" And the child is to answer: "Since nothing is held by faith except what contributes to the consolation of the souls of the pious." Only what "contributes to the consolation of the souls of the pious"! Not exactly a child's language, but the point is clear: Hell is not an edifying subject—not for young minds.

But what of *adult* minds? Well, they perhaps should be better able to ask what truth gave rise to the frightening image of unquenchable flames, and how it can stand alongside the fundamental Christian belief that the Landlord is "very, very kind." The decline of the old belief in a physical hell cannot allow us to leave every thought of judgment unheeded. Much of the medieval imagery of hell has no direct basis in our Bibles, and we are not bound to keep it forever. But the unquenchable fire does! It was one of the images used to foretell the coming of the Savior. Which brings me to our second theme: *judgment withheld.*

II

The one who prepared the way for Christ, in fulfillment of Old Testament prophecy (Mal. 4:5; Matt. 11:14), was John the Baptist. John did not expect the "Day of the Lord" to be merely the rescue of Israel from her oppressors; like Amos (Amos 5:18), he foresaw it as a day when Israel herself would be judged. He spoke of the wrath to come, and warned that whereas he himself baptized with water, the one who was to come would baptize with the fire of judgment. John pictured the Coming One as a farmer, who, when the wheat has been threshed, tosses the wheat and chaff into the air to separate out the grain. "The chaff he will burn with unquenchable fire" (Matt. 3:12).

The image of the farmer with winnowing fork in hand is a vivid and powerful one. But does it fit Jesus of Nazareth? That's the question. True, Jesus could speak a harsh word on occasion; but he did not bring about the judgment John had expected. The impression Jesus made, when he came into Galilee preaching the gospel of the kingdom, was not at all like John the Baptist's grim figure of power and doom. No Old Testament image fit Jesus better than that of the "suffering servant," of whom Isaiah wrote that he would not raise his voice in the streets and would not break a bruised reed or put out a smoldering wick (Matt. 12:19–20).

Jesus, when he came, pronounced his woes on the scribes and Pharisees (Matthew 23). But he lamented over Jerusalem, and chose an image for himself that stood in striking contrast to the expectations of John the Baptist: "Jerusalem, Jerusalem . . . How often have I desired to gather your children together as a hen gathers her brood under her wings, and you were not willing!" (Matt. 23:37).

The baptism with fire seems to have been withheld, and it is no wonder that John the Baptist sent his perplexed inquiry from prison: "Are you he who is to come, or are we to wait for another?" (Matt. 11:3). John did not live to see the most astonishing reversal of all: instead of the severe judgment that John foresaw, it was Jesus himself who was put on trial, found guilty, and put to death.

III

Then is there no divine judgment at all? The answer is in my text: We have to consider, thirdly, a *judgment unintended*, but real nonetheless. As that other John, John the Evangelist, reflects on Jesus' words to Nicodemus, he sees that even a revelation of purest love makes a division among us, between those who discern it and those who turn their eyes from the light. Judgment was not the purpose of Christ's mission, but it was in fact one result of it. For "this is the judgment, that the light has come into the world, and people loved darkness rather than light."

But if this is the judgment, then everything looks different in its light. The lifting up of the Savior on the cross does not seem at all like the exaltation of a king in glory; but in fact it draws everyone to Christ, and so it is the judgment of the world (John 12:31–32). The sentence is not in the far-off future, at the end of time; it is now (John 12:31), and those who do not see with the eyes of faith are sentenced already (John 3:18). It is not God or Christ who sentences them; we all judge ourselves by what we make of the cross.

And what is the penalty for unbelief? It is not that we condemn ourselves to be cast into the flames of a literal hell, but that we choose to live without the fullness of God's love in Christ. The judgment, as Bishop Westcott (Brooke Foss Westcott; 1825–1901) says, is "not an arbitrary sentence but the working out of an absolute law."

The gravest problem with the old "fire and brimstone" preaching was that it assumed an impossible contradiction in the nature of God: if the sinner did not choose to have the *love* of God, he or she had to have the *justice* of God.

Jonathan Edwards (1703–58), in his famous sermon "Sinners in the Hands of an Angry God," warned the unconverted in his congregation how excellent God's love is, but how terrible God's wrath. God, he said, abhorred them and held them over the pit of hell "much as one holds a spider, or some loathsome insect, over the fire." And they would be tormented in the presence of the Lamb.

John the Evangelist, by contrast, though he knows of God's wrath (3:36), teaches the profound truth that the judgment has its source in God's love, if we turn away from it; and our turning away from it is its own sufficient penalty.

If I disparage some great work of art, the judgment turns back on myself, and I deprive myself of something of value.

When Mephistopheles makes his first appearance in Marlowe's play, Faustus asks him why, if he is in truth a devil, he is not in hell. Mephistopheles answers: "Why this is hell, nor am I out of it." He has deprived himself of the presence of God. That is his hell.

A wise Christian was asked how God, if God is merciful, could deprive anyone of the kingdom. He answered: "Why do you keep moving your head?" "Because the sun gets in my eyes," was the reply. And the saint remarked: "Exactly. God doesn't keep anyone out of the kingdom, but there are some who cannot bear the light."

"This is the judgment, that the light has come into the world, and people loved darkness rather than light." I would not venture to claim that this is all the New Testament says about judgment. But it surely is what is most important. It carries our thoughts back to the unquenchable flame of which John the Evangelist wrote in the prologue to his Gospel: "The light shines in the darkness, and the darkness has not overcome it" (1:5, RSV).

Running the Race

*"Since we are surrounded by so great a cloud
of witnesses, let us . . . run with perserverance the
race that is set before us, looking to Jesus the
pioneer and perfecter of our faith."*
Hebrews 12:1–2

We know very little about the writer of these famous
words. As long ago as the third century C.E., one of the
early Christian fathers wisely said: "As to who wrote this
epistle, God alone knows the truth" (Origen). Neither do
we know much about the people to whom he wrote—no
more, really, than we can infer from the letter itself. But
it is clear enough that the author addressed the themes of
faith and perseverance to Christians who bore the cross of
persecution and were tempted to give up. The worst,
apparently, was already over: physical abuse (Heb.
10:32–34) had given way to unpopularity and contempt,
and the author reminds the readers that none of them had
yet paid for their faith with their blood (12:2–4). They
were tired of the cross of shame, of humiliation. They
needed to recall those heroes of old, and the Savior himself, who had suffered torture and even death in order to
keep the faith.

Persecution is hardly our problem, even in its milder
form. On the other hand, in our learned community we
don't exactly prize faith, or reward belief as a virtue. All
the merit among us goes to the questioning, critical, in-
quiring mind, and we rightly think that education has a
great deal to do with what Sebastian Castellio (1515–63)
called the "art of doubting." Not faith, but doubt—there
is the academy's highest virtue. And the two can easily run

into conflict, the habit of believing and the habit of prob-
ing, questioning, taking nothing for granted.

The scholar and the scientist, it seems, have a heavy
cross to bear if they want to be Christians. Has the Letter
to the Hebrews anything to say to us about the cross of
doubt? I think so—if there is to be but one Christian faith
for the learned and the unlearned alike. And I, for one,
could not call myself a churchman if I thought it were otherwise. Scholars and scientists are not called to a higher
faith, and they don't have to settle for a lower faith, than
everyone else. Genuine faith is not peculiar to just one variety of Christian. Neither is doubt.

"In all of us," John Calvin (1509–64) says, "faith is always mingled with incredulity." Miguel de Unamuno
(1864–1936) says: "Faith which does not doubt is dead
faith." They are right. Unamuno may even have been
right when he said that there is a sacred doubt which is the
"mother of true faith." Like sickness and bereavement,
then, doubt is something you can expect and should prepare for, not letting it surprise you like the thief in the
night. Otherwise, there may come a day when your most
cherished beliefs will have to stand some test of life or
thought with which they are not equipped to deal.

None of you, I suspect, has in fact escaped those disturbing moments in which Martin Luther's (1483–1546)
question interrupts your thoughts: "Who knows whether
it is so?" Are the beliefs we heard from our parents, or
learned in church, or copied into our notebooks really
true? Even if faith wins the victory at such moments,
things are never quite the same again. From then on, faith
is "mingled with incredulity."

Don't feel guilty about it! Remember that the church,
in its wisdom, has kept that strange, unnerving book Ecclesiastes at the very heart of the canon of sacred Scripture. There it stands as an inescapable symbol of the incredulity that breaks into the citadel of faith. It is the No
of doubt against which the Yes of faith must always struggle—that other, cheerless possibility that the little act of
human existence may have no meaning. "Whatever your
hand finds to do, do with your might; for there is no work

or thought or knowledge or wisdom in Sheol, to which you are going" (Eccl. 9:10).

In Ecclesiastes, the detached, critical intellect pays a high price as it applies itself to wisdom. I hope it is not significant that the author's title, *Qoheleth*, is sometimes translated "the Professor," or I may be addressing a problem I have myself helped to create in the exercise of my professional duties.

So, what is it that my text has to say to Ecclesiastes? At least three things. They are obvious enough, I suppose. But it is often neglect of the obvious that turns the virtue of doubt into denial of the virtue of faith.

I

First: "*Since we are surrounded by so great a cloud of witnesses . . .*" This means that faith is not a lonely struggle: we believe, and we doubt, in good company.

True, the witnesses cannot believe *for* us. There is no belief by proxy. As Luther taught us, all must do their own believing, as all must do their own dying. Even the church cannot relieve us of the responsibility for our own faith.

Neither can we point to the faith of the church as though it afforded a knockdown proof of the reality of God. The writer of the Letter to the Hebrews has no "argument from religious experience," though it does help, when we fall into doubt, to have our eyes opened to see the horses and chariots of the Lord. They that be for us, if not more than those that be against us, are many (2 Kings 6:16–17). Or, as C. D. Broad (1887–1971), the coolest of Cambridge philosophers, put it less poetically: "The claim of any particular religion or sect to have complete or final truth . . . seems to me to be too ridiculous to be worth a moment's consideration. But the opposite extreme of holding that the whole religious experience of mankind is a gigantic system of pure delusion seems to me to be almost (though not quite) as farfetched."

Still, we point to the cloud of witnesses neither to believe for us, nor to guarantee the object of our belief, but simply in recognition of a fact: that the assurance of faith, if we ever had it, came to us from the company of believers; and if we have it still, that is most likely because the company continues to support and sustain us.

There is nothing so very mysterious about this fact. In any department of human experience, the final test by which we allow ourselves, however unconsciously, to accept one thing as "truth" and to reject another thing as "error" is the existence of a group that shares our conviction. We learn the language of the guild, another team reproduces our experiment; the conviction is shared, and we are reassured. Doubt becomes disaster when it makes us withdraw into ourselves and cut ourselves off from that communion of saints that is the Mother of the faithful.

Of course, our author meant by his "cloud of witnesses" the great believers of the past. But they form one company with the witnesses of the present, many of whom (sadly) will "have no memorial" (Sir. [Ecclus.] 44:9, RSV). It was the living saints that Luther had in mind when he exclaimed: "The church's faith supports my fearfulness." He understood very well that while the saints past and present cannot offer us a treasury of merits to be transferred to our account, they do afford a treasury of faith to strengthen our uncertainty.

You may object that if my brother and sister, too, have their doubts, what can they offer me but more uncertainty? The answer is that shared doubts—like confessed sins—lose their power over us. Even to admit our doubts to one another has a strange efficacy to confirm our faith, or make it a better faith. And if in our pride or our timidity we shun the fellowship, what can we say but: "O God, in your mercy, plague us with more doubts until we turn again"?

II

Second: "*Looking to Jesus, the pioneer and perfecter of our faith* . . ." Our faith, if it is Christian faith, is a gift of grace, and our responsibility for it can never be more than a responsibility to receive it gladly and gratefully.

You would not thank me if I now launched into a discourse on grace and free will. I simply appeal to what every Christian knows in his or her heart: that to be a believer at all is to be vanquished by the grace of Christ. We do not say in our prayers: "Lord, we make a fine partnership, you and I." We say with the Apostle Paul: "By the grace of God I am what I am, and his grace toward me has not been in vain" (1 Cor. 15:10).

But how is faith a gift of grace? What can that possibly mean? The answer of the Letter to the Hebrews is clear: faith is given to us as we are drawn into the story of him who is the "pioneer and perfecter of faith." Not that everything we hear in the gospel is easy to believe or understand. It is interesting that the disciples said, "Lord, to whom can we go? You have the words of eternal life" (John 6:68) just after they had expressed total puzzlement at what Jesus was saying. Many of them left him. Others stayed. The faith-giving company of Jesus is not reserved for those who understand and believe all that he says; it is open to all who are drawn irresistibly to him by the intuition that here are words of life, and who can at least say: "I believe; help my unbelief!" (Mark 9:24).

And it is not just his words that impart the gift of faith. It is precisely his story, which is a story of faith assailed by doubt. In him too faith was "mingled with incredulity"; he was no exception to Calvin's rule. Despite unflinching obedience to his Father's will, he could meet the apparent senselessness of the cross only with an agonized "Why?" "My God, my God, why have you forsaken me?" (Mark 15:34). But his doubt was included in his faith, and he died, we are told, with a simple confession of trust: "Father, into your hands I commend my spirit" (Luke 23:46). That's how he gives the gift of faith even to doubters—because he himself is the archetype of faith assailed by doubt.

III

Third and last: "*Let us run with perseverance the race that is set before us.*" Faith is not so much a belief to be entertained, or a case to be proved; it is a life to be lived, a race to be run. This is the metaphor that pervades the entire passage. The cloud of witnesses are rows upon rows of spectators in the stadium; they are watching us, and urging us on, as we run the race they have completed. And the writer evidently pictures Jesus himself, who has also finished the course, waiting at the finish line.

Something utterly crucial is at stake here. Faith, as the New Testament speaks of it, does not conjure up an image of professors in their studies trying out arguments, but of athletes in the stadium or stewards in the vineyard. If faith were justified only by proofs, then only those with a university degree would be capable of it, or, at least, they alone could have the right to believe. But the truth is that the "conviction of things not seen" (Heb. 11:1) comes to those, whether learned or unlearned, who run the race—which is why it calls for perseverance more than for argument.

We are not likely to underestimate thought in a university environment. But thinking is not our only contact with truth. Doing puts us in touch with reality too—more directly and convincingly perhaps than anything else does or can. Whatever may be the case with other kinds of faith, *religious* faith is *practical* belief.

Back in 1986, I read in a magazine article from England the life story of a devout woman I had known when I was a student but had not spoken with for more than thirty years. Brought up in a believing household, Gladys had seen both her brothers ordained to the Anglican priesthood. No such way of witnessing to her Lord was open to her in those days. The paper quotes her as saying: "I don't know why I didn't marry, like every other girl. It just didn't happen."

Had she married, her story would have been very different. At the age of seventy-four, she was celebrating (as the article so nicely put it) "the recent arrival of her two hundredth child"—a baby boy with Down's syndrome. In the space of forty-two years, she had opened her modest home to two hundred unwanted, handicapped, lost, battered, and orphaned children, whose photographs filled every inch of her living room.

I tracked down Gladys's phone number the next time I

was in England and called her. She answered the phone herself and said immediately (after more than thirty years, mind you!): "Ah, Brian! I pray for you every year on your birthday." I doubt if Gladys has ever come up with a good argument to stop the mouth of an infidel who proclaims that all is vanity and it makes no difference what you do. But she has her memorial. She is one of the great cloud of witnesses, and she can surely claim as she looks back on her life: "I have fought the good fight, I have finished the race, I have kept the faith" (2 Tim. 4:7).

Justice

"Let justice roll down like waters,
and righteousness like an ever flowing stream."
Amos 5:24

Amos may be easier to respect and admire than to love. The moral power of his message leaps out of the pages of the Old Testament. It created a masterpiece of ancient literature, and we can hardly believe that behind all the eloquence and penetrating insight stands a herdsman and part-time gardener. But the word he speaks is profoundly disturbing. It is a stinging rebuke, and Amos stands over against his listeners with a frigid, accusing eye.

I

An honest countryman, he came to the big city, didn't like what he found, and said so in no uncertain terms. He was an outsider who could not feel—as Hosea did—for the pitiful weakness of sinners. He spoke from his lofty eminence above them, not from among them or beside them.

You wouldn't expect him to be popular. No doubt the people said to Amos what, according to him, they said to all the prophets: "Prophesy not!" (Amos 2:12, KJV). We don't want to hear you, they say. And Amos replied that the prophet does not *choose* to prophesy, and he cannot *choose* to stop. It is as simple as the law of cause and effect in nature. The prey is cornered; the lion roars. The lion roars; the people shudder. The Lord speaks—who can but prophesy? (3:8).

Even the "clergy"—especially the clergy—complained about Amos. "The land is not able to bear all his words"

(7:10). They tried to have him removed for treason, because he predicted the fall of the king and the destruction
of Israel (vv. 10–11). Amaziah the priest warned Amos to
his face that he had better go earn his living somewhere
else—in Judah, where he came from. Amos replied that he
was not one of your professional seers ("no prophet, nor
a prophet's son"); he spoke because the Lord had called
him. And, in a ferocious prediction, he told Amaziah that
in the coming disaster the priest's own wife would be
forced into prostitution, his sons and daughters would be
killed, and Amaziah himself would be dragged off to die
in exile (vv. 16–17).

Disaster did come. In 722 B.C.E. the armies of Assyria
crossed the border into Israel, and in 721 B.C.E. the kingdom of Israel no longer existed. But the sting in the
prophet's message was not only that he foretold a catastrophe; the sting lay in the reason he gave for its coming:
because a flourishing religion had taken a wrong turn.
This is what gives his prophecy a meaning that transcends
ancient history.

I do not wish, like Amos, to proclaim a great national
apostasy, much less to predict a national catastrophe. But
I do believe that Amos challenges us too, like the ancient
Israelites, to scrutinize our own religion, to ask whether it
pleases the God we worship as much as it pleases us. The
Israelites did not want to hear the prophet's question. And
it may not be what we Americans would most like to hear
either—unless we have acquired that wonderful art of so
identifying ourselves with the Lord's prophets that we see
the moral failure they castigate only out there, in others,
none of it within ourselves. In any case, unpopular questions have their place.

II

The angry denunciations Amos poured out give us a
vivid picture of a nation in a postwar period (under Jer-
oboam II). The country had been engaged in a costly war
(with Syria), which at first had gone badly. But the tide
turned, and after victory came unparalleled prosperity. As

he made his way through the land, Amos noted the signs of affluence. He observed a people living well and eating well. It was like nothing the nation had ever known before.

There were magnificent homes with paneled rooms, tables loaded with delicacies, and a happy round of social events. Amos was impressed that many families even had their summer homes as well as their winter homes.

He noticed, too, that the people, on the whole, were very religious. The great national shrines were crowded with worshipers. Organized religion shared in the affluence of its adherents. And people gave generously to support the religion of their choice.

Indeed, the nation was persuaded that its success and prosperity were sure tokens of God's special favor. Hence there was a confidence and a security in the land. People looked forward to a still brighter future—to the "Day of the Lord," the even better time coming.

But there was more to it than that. Amos uncovered another, darker side of the picture. Not all Israel shared in the new affluence. There was the *other* Israel—a people in need. And when they cried for justice, they found that justice costs money, which they didn't have. (That's why they needed justice.)

The affluent, for the most part, were totally indifferent. They turned aside from the needy. The leaders of the nation, to whom the poor brought their urgent appeal, remained complacent and were not sickened by the nation's wounds.

Worse still, there were some who deliberately exploited the poor, overcharging them and selling them short measure. They fixed the scales in which the merchandise was weighed. With the good produce they mixed trash that the rich refused to buy. And though they religiously closed shop on the Sabbath, they spent the day thinking only of the almighty shekel and tomorrow's profits.

The poor could fall more and more deeply into debt until their worth was no more than the price of a pair of shoes.

Finally, Amos noted that the affluence had its darker side even for those who had it. It led to a weakening of the moral fiber, to self-indulgence, immoderate drinking, and sexual permissiveness.

III

So, what was the message of Amos? Well, Amos was no country bumpkin: he was a blunt man, but he was also shrewd. He knew how to win a favorable hearing. His prophecy starts off by listing the sins of *other* nations. And we can be sure his audience loved it.

He had heard that in the wicked world outside there were captive nations; brutal governments; callous politicians who cynically made and broke meaningless treaties; armies that extended a nation's boundaries over the dead bodies of women and children. Amos announced the judgment of God on all those un-Israelite activities. And you can almost hear the congregation shout, "Amen!"

But then he turns to *Israel,* lists its sins, and adds: "Hear this word that the LORD has spoken against *you,* O people of Israel. . . . You only have I known of all the families of the earth; therefore I will *punish* you for all your iniquities" (3:1–2). You too! Indeed, you especially! Israel is specially favored, but that only increases its guilt—and God's anger. Not charity, but judgment, begins at home.

The Day of the Lord—the day they are cheerfully awaiting—the Day of the Lord is darkness, and not light (5:18). When God comes to visit Israel, it will be to destroy the altars erected in God's honor.

The message of Amos is quite simply this: God takes no pleasure in men and women who religiously pay homage in the sanctuary, if they do not strive to right the wrongs of the world outside. God refuses to hear their liturgies, the prayers they offer, the hymns they sing. God demands that the earth be flooded with justice.

> "I hate, I despise your feasts,
>   and I take no delight in your solemn assemblies.
> . . . .
>   let justice roll down like waters,
> and righteousness like an everflowing stream."
>   (5:21, 24 RSV)

"Justice"—that, in one word, is the message of Amos, to be repeated as forcefully, but not so single-mindedly, by the later prophets of Judah. "Bringing offerings is futile," says the God of Isaiah: "Seek justice, rescue the oppressed" (Isa. 1:13, 17). "What does the LORD require of you," asks Micah, "but to do justice, and to love kindness, and to walk humbly with your God?" (Micah 6:8).

And a stunning message it is! A God who cares about nothing so much as justice! The historian Herodotus (c. 484–425 B.C.E.) speaks for the greater part of the ancient world when he observes that "divinity is all a matter of jealousy." The relationship of humanity to God is governed, in the mind of Herodotus, by the thought that the immortals are jealous for their prerogatives: they will cut down anyone who challenges their dignity or neglects to pay them homage, but they can be bought off with bribes.

Olympus is thus another self-interested stratum of an unequal society; and religion, in this view, is a matter of human prudence—of humanity's self-interest. For Amos, by total contrast, divinity is synonymous not with jealousy, but with justice. To seek the Lord is not to pay your "sacrificial tolls," but to seek the good. Religion addresses not our self-interest, but our conscience. The Day of the Lord is not the Good Time Coming, but the time of reckoning. When the day comes, it is justice that finally counts, cutting across all the other things we treasure—even our religion—and relativizing them with its absolute moral demand. God is not pulled down into a corrupt society as another participant in the struggle for domination; God is absolutely sovereign over it, and, one way or another, its inequities will be redressed.

It was a stunning message in Amos's day. . . . It still is in *our* day.

IV

Perhaps it is post–World War II America, rather than post-Vietnam America, that you will see mirrored in the prophecy of Amos—the America, let's say, of John Foster Dulles (1888–1959), when the dollar was sound, the country was sublimely confident of its military might and its special mission, and there was a religious awakening that was the envy of the European churches.

With the civil rights movement, the other America—the America of economic, social, and political deprivation—became more visible. And with the Vietnam War, the national sense of purpose faltered, prosperity weakened.

Our own prophets of doom warned us in the 1960s that we live in a postmodern age, in which religion will gradually die out. Their predictions have proved less reliable than those of Amos. And we now hear of a resurgence of patriotism, prosperity, and religion, in a post-postmodern age. But what kind of religion? Is it the religion of Amos?

I have read in a publication of my own Presbyterian Church that our Reformer, John Calvin (1509–64), was principally interested in salvation; and that, apart from evangelism, "all of the other matters in which we as a denomination involve ourselves [merely] duplicate the efforts of secular agencies." It is not that the author denies the importance of the "great social issues" on which his church, like others, has taken a public stand. But he thinks we've got our priorities wrong, and that it isn't the church's duty to take over the lesser tasks.

He accuses evangelism-shy Presbyterians of hiding behind their social concerns. No doubt that is possible, whenever the roots of Christian social action in the gospel are forgotten. But I notice that the prophet Amos was worried about the other possibility—that social indifference may hide behind a self-centered piety. The church, surely, is in serious trouble if either evangelism or social action is perceived as the main, or even exclusive, business of the church, as though the two were somehow competing goals.

And what does Calvin have to say? I don't know what texts my fellow Presbyterian may have had in mind. But in my Calvin I do find this:

> There is no man imbued with true piety who will not
> consider it poor taste to give a long and detailed ex-
> hortation to aspire after heaven. That appeals to a man
> wholly preoccupied with himself. . . . It is the duty of a
> Christian man to ascend higher than merely to seek
> and secure the salvation of his soul. . . . It is not very
> sound theology to confine a man's thoughts so much to
> himself, and not to set before him as the prime motive
> of his existence zeal to display the glory of God.

That leaves us in no doubt about John Calvin's priorities.
Of course, he was interested in individual salvation, but he
evidently thought it possible to overrate the quest for it.
His prime question was not: "How can I be saved?" but
"What must be done for the honor of God?" And no one
will doubt that he included a just society among the things
that glorify God—and therefore among the most urgent
concerns of those who profess to be saved.

More to the point: the Savior himself reaffirms the religion of Amos when he says: "Woe to you Pharisees! For
you . . . neglect justice" (Luke 11:42; Matt. 23:23). And for
the Savior, too, the crucial question on the Day of Judgment is: What did you do for the hungry, the thirsty, the
stranger, the unclothed, the sick, the captive? (Matt.
25:31–46).

But I have also read—not once, but many times—that
while social justice is of course a prime concern for the individual Christian, it is not a collective task for the church.
The question is then not one of priorities, but of policy or
strategy. In part, this opinion rests on the feeling of many
devout church people that their leadership has let them
down by an unwise use of the church's money and influence—from the denominational level all the way up to the
World Council of Churches.

Sometimes, I fear, the charges have been well founded.
But I think Roy Larson got it exactly right when he wrote
that for all their failures, the World Council of Churches
and the National Council of Churches *have* "fed the hungry, clothed the naked, cared for the sick, sheltered the
homeless, . . . served as authentic voices for the powerless."

And I wonder: Would all these things have happened if no collective means for justice were available to overcome collective injustice? Wrong has a head start over right. If you don't like the World Council of Churches, have you, realistically, a third alternative between being ineffectual or putting your money on an organization you *do* trust?

The trickle-down of goodwill from the individual Christian is no substitute for the "mighty stream" (KJV).

> Let justice roll down like waters,
> > and righteousness like an everflowing stream.

The Proof of Friendship

*"You are my friends if you do
what I command you."*
John 15:14

This is surely one of the most remarkable things the New
Testament tells us about Jesus and his followers. He calls
them, not servants, but *friends.* There is another place, in
Luke, where he names them "my friends" (Luke 12:4),
and in the very moment of betrayal he addresses even Judas as "friend" (Matt. 26:50). But more familiar to most of
us, I daresay, is the Apostle Paul's theme: Not servants,
but *children.* "So you are no longer a slave but a child, and
if a child then also an heir, through God" (Gal. 4:7). "You
did not receive a spirit of slavery to fall back into fear": the
Spirit bears witness "that we are children of God" (Rom.
8:15–16).

"Friends" and "children." Is there any real difference
between these two ways of speaking? Or any reason that
we might find one more helpful than the other?

The image of the believer as a son or daughter of God
has proved itself wonderfully fruitful in Christian literature. It has the power to shatter the hard yoke of the law,
which keeps the slave or servant in a constant state of anxiety. The servant must get the assignment done, and must
get it right. But children, as John Calvin (1509–64) says,
do not hesitate to show their father unfinished assignments, or even assignments they have spoiled a little,
trusting that he will accept them anyway. "And we need
this assurance in no small measure," he adds, "because
without it we attempt everything in vain. . . . Who can
manage amid all those terrors of uncertainty whether God
is offended or honored by our work?"

With the image of our adoption as sons and daughters of God goes the picture of Christ as brother (Rom. 8:29), who is not ashamed to call God's other children his brothers and sisters (Heb. 2:11; cf. v. 17). This, too, is rooted in the Gospel story. Jesus called the inner circle of his disciples "my brothers" (Matt. 28:10; John 20:17), and all who sat around him his "brothers" and "sisters" (Matt. 12:49; Mark 3:33; Luke 8:19–21). Calvin liked to complete the family, so to say, by speaking of Christ as the older brother who takes us by the hand into the Father's presence. Not servants, then, but sons and daughters of God, and therefore brothers and sisters of Christ. It is a powerful and attractive image.

But many will feel that the image of friendship suggests an even greater warmth and intimacy, and they have Scripture on their side. The book of Proverbs says, "A true friend is closer . . . than a brother" (Prov. 18:24, Anchor Bible)—or, as the older versions have it, a friend "sticks closer than a brother" (RSV). Of course, you don't have to make a choice between Christ the friend and Christ the older brother. But friendship, too, is a theme with a rich history in Christian literature, and in classical literature as well. It is worth looking at as carefully as the other, perhaps more familiar theme.

It was a common saying in ancient Greece that friendship implies equality. Not that friendship is only possible between equals. But it is a great equalizer in the sense that it overcomes differences of status. Cicero (106–43 B.C.E.) thought this was the greatest thing about friendship—that by it those who are superior put themselves on the level of those lower down. That, however, to his mind, does not abolish differences of intelligence, wealth, or social standing. How could it?

Some such notion of friendship is what we need if we are to understand our gospel lesson correctly. By his friendship Jesus really did, in a sense, put himself on the level of his disciples. But there is not the slightest suggestion that this made them equals. He remained the Master, and they remained the disciples. It is an intimate, even mutual relationship, without actual equality. And the

heart of the matter is in verse 14: "You are my friends if
you do what I command you." Each half of the text calls
for a closer look.

I

"*You are my friends. . . .*" One thing must be said plainly
at the outset. It would subvert the entire message of the
Gospel if we made the second half of the text a prior condition of the first. The meaning is not: You do as I command you first; then, and only then, will I take you for my
friends. The disciples *are* Christ's friends. He is speaking
to them about abiding in his love, which they already
have, and his discourse moves from the allegory of the
vine to the new name for his disciples: "I am the vine, you
are the branches [v. 5]. . . . You are my friends."

It is true that Jesus does not say "*I* am *your* friend," either here or anywhere else—just as in the Old Testament
we find Abraham as the friend of God, but no express
statement that God is Abraham's friend (2 Chron. 20:7;
Isa. 41:8; cf. James 2:23). It may be the inequality of the
relationship that we should infer from this one-sided us-
age. Still, mutuality is seldom absent from the thought of
"being friends" (cf. Ps. 25:14), and it seems clearly to be
present when we read: "The LORD used to speak to Moses
face to face, as one speaks to a friend" (Ex. 33:11). And
Jesus' enemies were not mistaken when they called him,
albeit in mockery, the "friend of tax collectors and sinners" (Matt. 11:19; Luke 7:34). That was the scandal of his
ministry, that he sat at table with sinners (Matt. 9:10–12;
Mark 2:15–17; Luke 5:29–32). *They* were his friends; *he*
was their friend.

We have every right, then, to understand the first half
of our text in the light of whatever the Scriptures teach us
elsewhere about the meaning of friendship. To begin
with, there is much to learn from what is said about the
persistent failure of human friendship. There are *sham*
friends, like those who surround a person of wealth and
influence, for the rich have many friends, and everyone is
friend to a giver of gifts (Prov. 14:20; 19:4, 6). There are

opinionated friends, ever ready to increase your misery by giving you their homespun philosophies, as Job found out (Job 2:11; 6:27; 19:14). There are *fair-weather* friends, no longer around when you actually need them (Ps. 38:11). There are *fainthearted* friends, who let the least whisper of idle gossip come between them (Prov. 16:28). There is the *self-righteous, virtuous* friend, who, when you need forgiveness, won't let you forget (Prov. 17:9). And, saddest of all, there is the *unfaithful* friend, who betrays your trust: "Even my bosom friend in whom I trusted,/who ate of my bread, has lifted the heel against me" (Ps. 41:9).

We could put together a good picture of the ideal friend simply by turning these negative descriptions around. But the positive is already there. The *true* friend loves at all times, no matter what (Prov. 17:17). The *true* friend is there when you fall, to pick you up (Eccl. 4:9–10). Even the rebuke of a *true* friend is an act of friendship, for "well meant are the wounds a friend inflicts" (Prov. 27:6). Like good wine, friendship gets better with age (Sir. 9:10), and yet the *true* friend is ready even to surrender life itself for you: there is no "greater love than this, to lay down one's life for one's friends" (John 15:13; cf. Rom. 5:8; 1 John 3:16).

"You are my friends." All of this is what the first half of our text means. The final proof of Jesus' friendship for the disciples was his readiness even to die for them. The proof of *their* friendship for *him* comes in the second half of the text.

II

"You are my friends *if you do what I command you.*" The proof of being a friend to Christ, it turns out, is no different than the proof of being his brothers and sisters. "Whoever does the will of God is my brother and sister and mother" (Mark 3:35). Or, as Luke's version has it, "My mother and my brothers are those who hear the word of God and do it" (Luke 8:21). Just so: "You are my friends if you do what I command you."

The image of God or Christ as friend appeals to us

because it suggests a more mature and responsible relationship than God as our king and father, or Christ as lord and master. We are not just told to be good children and obedient servants. Still, we dare not fail to notice that in the Gospel reading (John 15:14) Jesus speaks of *obedient* friends. The difference from being just an obedient servant is that servants are kept in the dark: they get the day's assignment and do as they are told, whether anxiously (as Calvin imagined) or indifferently (with one eye on the clock). The friends of Christ are not less, but more obedient, because it has been given to them to understand and love him. They actually care about his commandments, and not about their rewards. But in case they forget, he reminds them (in verse 20): "Remember the word that I said to you, 'Servants are not greater than their master.'"

One risk with the image of friendship, precious though it is, is that it may betray us into a kind of contentment and self-satisfaction that neither gives Christ his due nor takes us out of ourselves. When Crocodile Dundee explains, "Me an' God—we be pals," we may envy him his familiarity with the Creator, but still wonder if he has his theology right—whether God has in fact become an idol small enough to slip into the pocket of his bush jacket. *Your God Is Too Small* was the title of a provocative little book by J. B. Phillips, better known as a Bible translator. It is still worth reading. In Christ we have what Phillips calls a "focused God." But he is not any smaller: he still speaks with divine authority. And many of his friends— Paul, James, and Peter, to name a few—never ceased to style themselves "a servant of Jesus Christ" (Rom. 1:1; James 1:1; 2 Peter 1:1).

". . . if you do what I command you." Actually, the Master gives us only one commandment—to love. He called it "new," though in itself it is at least as old as Leviticus 19:18. What was new about it was that his friends were to love one another as *he* loved *them* (John 13:34), which must mean at least this: extending *his* friendship to one another, being there for one another even if it costs. It is much harder than we usually admit to set aside self-interest in friendship. Epictetus (c. 55–c. 135) asks: "Did you never see dogs fawning on one another and playing with one another, so that you say: 'Nothing could be more friendly'? But to see what their friendship amounts to, throw a piece of meat between them and you will find out." Christ's commandment demands more than that.

Another difficulty we have is that we tend to draw the limits of friendship too narrowly. Indeed, Aristotle remarks: "To be a friend to many people . . . is not possible; just as you cannot be in love with many at once." It has been alleged that even the picture of Jesus himself in the Fourth Gospel does not rise above the narrow limits of love between friends. The Jesus of Luke's Gospel, by contrast, tells us not to invite our friends for dinner, but "the poor, the crippled, the lame, and the blind" (Luke 14:12–14). We can be grateful that we have both Gospels. But, surely, if God's love is for the world, as John 3:16 says, the love of Jesus and his friends is not intended to be anything less. This, too, we must recognize in his commandment.

III

Well, you may have the uneasy feeling by now that in my comments on part two of my text I have taken something away from my comments on the first part, since I have moved from the self-giving of the Savior to demands, demands, demands. Is something taken away from the intimacy and warmth of his friendship if his commanding will is what we return to? For many people, all talk of commandments is forbidding, like the thunder and lightning of Sinai (Ex. 19:16). But in actual fact the divine imperative comes to us as the voice of purest love and friendship.

F. W. Robertson (1816–53) recalled from his own experience that dark night of the soul in which every support begins to crumble beneath it, until nothing seems left to believe in. Supposed friends only frown, bid one to stifle the offending doubts; and they shrink back uncomprehendingly. If Robertson is right, the one and only thing that can pull you through is the simple but inescapable moral imperative.

> In the darkest hour through which a human soul can
> pass, whatever else is doubtful, this at least is certain. If
> there be no God, and no future state, yet, even then, it
> is better to be generous than selfish, better to be chaste
> than licentious, better to be true than false, better to be
> brave than to be a coward.

For Robertson himself, at any rate, this final source of order amid the chaos was the way back to the God and the
Christ he had lost.

It is, of course, the teaching of Christ that we cannot be
trusted to listen to the inner voice; we stand in need of
repentance, forgiveness, and grace. But the fact that he
reawakens the divine imperative within is in itself further
proof of his friendship: we know him as friend not least in
his commandment, by which he bids us share his joy in
doing God's will. "I have said these things to you so that
my joy may be in you, and that your joy may be complete"
(John 15:11).

Companions

The Real Treasure of the Church

(Reformation Day)

*"I do not account my life of any value nor as precious
to myself, if only I may accomplish my course and
the ministry which I received from the Lord Jesus,
to testify to the gospel of the grace of God."*
Acts 20:24

When I had occasion to travel around Lake Ontario in
Canada and upstate New York, I remembered that I was
in the territory of James Fenimore Cooper's (1789–1851)
fearless hero, the scout "Hawkeye." Although I hadn't
read the "Leatherstocking Tales" for more than thirty
years, two incidents that have always been linked in my
own imagination, if not in the author's intention, kept
coming back to me. When I reached home again, a little
scouting of my own amid the boxes piled up in the base-
ment uncovered the volume I was looking for: *The
Pathfinder* (1840). Helped by my old pencil marks in the
margins and inside the covers, I soon found the two passages I was after. And it occurred to me that they might
put us in the right frame of mind to think about Martin
Luther (1483–1546) and Reformation Day, and so the
gospel of the grace of God, which is what Luther's reformation was about.

I

The Pathfinder himself, Hawkeye, is of course the central character of the book, roaming the American wilderness like Adam in paradise before the Fall—honest,
rugged, uncomplicated. It is no accident that his given
name is *Nattie* Bumppo; like Nathanael in the Gospel he

is "an Israelite in whom there is no deceit" (John 1:47). Regrettably obliged to be a fighter, he knows that the important thing is to fight on the Lord's side, which he takes to mean on the side of His Majesty the king. He is convinced that all the good Indians fight for the British, and that those who fight for the French are vagabonds and "riptyles." A fascinating character! But I must admit that the character I found most intriguing in this particular tale was not Pathfinder but Charles Cap, the contentious mariner, who is sure that no inland lake can be compared with the Atlantic Ocean.

The first of my two incidents relates how Lake Ontario becomes the nemesis to Cap's pride. He has nothing but contempt for this bit of a pond, as he calls it, but he takes over the helm of the *Scud* anyway, in order to give the landlubbers a demonstration of seamanship. Caught in a violent storm, he is at first delighted to find himself wrestling with the elements once more. But then he realizes, to his dismay, that he cannot stop the boat from drifting inexorably to disaster on the breakers. "For the first time, most probably, since her keel had dipped into the limpid waters of Ontario, the voice of prayer was heard on board the *Scud*."

Reluctantly, Cap yields the helm to its usual master, who proceeds to steer directly at a bluff on the shore and skillfully uses the invisible undertow to keep the boat from foundering in a cauldron of breakers. The reverse current below counteracts the surface drift and keeps the anchor cables from parting. Cap admits that "this [blank] fresh water has an unnatural way with it" (expletive deleted). He is a saltwater sailor out of his element. As his niece Mabel has said to him earlier: "But Ontario is not your native element, dear uncle; for you come from the salt water while this is fresh."

The second incident has to do with religion, on which Cap is no less opinionated than he is on seamanship. Sergeant Dunham, Cap's brother and Mabel's father, has been mortally wounded and lies slowly dying in the blockhouse, without the din of battle to give him a soldier's courage in the face of death. Pathfinder reassures the sergeant that he has done his duty and may start his new journey with a light heart. But Mabel urges her father to rely on nothing he has done himself for mercy and salvation. She testifies to the gospel of the grace of God. Cap replies:

> Ay, ay, that's doctrine out of question. He will be our Judge, and keeps the log book of our acts, and will foot them all up at the last day, and then say who has done well and who has done ill. I do believe Mabel is right.

Cap misses the point entirely; that was not what Mabel meant at all. "Dearest father," she protests, "this is a vain illusion! Oh, place all your trust in the mediation of our Holy Redeemer." Cap simply hadn't grasped the meaning of "grace," which the theologians define as the "free, unmerited favor of God." You do nothing to earn it, but only hold out an empty hand to receive it as a gift.

Is it merely fanciful if I say: Poor Cap was out of his element again, not knowing how to sail his barque on what the French call "sweet water"? But if so, he was no more than the spokesman of us all, who live by the grace of God and can hardly believe it.

II

Cap's reaction to Mabel's words of comfort reminds me now, as it did when I first read it, of some things Luther said about hearing the gospel of grace. Take this, for instance:

> The human heart does not understand, nor does it believe, that so great a treasure as the Holy Spirit is given simply for the hearing of faith but argues like this: "It is a big thing—forgiveness of sins, deliverance from sin and death, the giving of the Holy Spirit, of righteousness and eternal life—so you must offer something big if you want to obtain those unspeakable gifts." This notion [Luther goes on] the Devil approves and fosters in the heart. And so when reason hears: "You cannot do a thing to obtain the forgiveness of sin except to hear the

word of God," it immediately cries out: "No, you make
the forgiveness of sins too mean and contemptible."
So, it is the very greatness of the gift that keeps us from
taking it, and because so great a treasure is given for
nothing, it is despised.

When it comes to the gospel of grace, "reason" is out of
its element like a saltwater mariner on Lake Ontario. It is
so hard for us to believe in free grace that we cannot simply reach out the empty hand and take the gift when it is
offered. The treasure is beyond our ability to grasp.

Remember what it was that first made Luther a reformer of the church. The men and women entrusted to
his pastoral care had been led to believe that there was a
treasury of merits from which they could draw to obtain
indulgences in return for their money. Christ himself had
established the treasury by his atoning work, so it was said,
and over the years the saints had added to it. Luther's
parishioners thought that when they received a certificate
of indulgence, they were literally buying forgiveness of
their sins, and they were ready to pay.

This is not what the church officially taught about indulgences, but it was what the indulgence mongers, like
Johann Tetzel (c. 1465–1519) led people to believe. In itself the idea of a treasury of merits contains a profound
truth: not one of us would be here today if it were not for
the great succession of saints who have added their labors
to the work of Christ. But that is something quite different from making merchandise of the gospel of grace. Tetzel is even reported to have said that those who had nothing on their consciences at the time, but had a mind to
commit a sin in the near future, could purchase their indulgence in advance. As a shepherd of the church, responsible for the welfare of his flock, Luther had to speak
out against Tetzel and his unscrupulous fund-raising.

The sum and substance of Luther's protest in the famous Ninety-five Theses (1517) is contained in Thesis
36, which states that every Christian who truly repents en-
joys full forgiveness of sins without the need for indulgences. But my favorite is Thesis 62: "The real treasure of

the church is the sacred gospel of the glory and grace of God." Not a treasury of merits for which one must pay, but the treasure of a grace that is free! That is the glory of God—grace. And what made Luther a reformer of the church was the amazing single-mindedness with which he testified to the absolute centrality of this word of grace. He could surely have said with the Apostle Paul (in the words of my text): "I do not account my life of any value nor as precious to myself, if only I may accomplish my course and the ministry which I received from the Lord Jesus, to testify to the gospel of the grace of God."

III

It may be that the Lutherans need no reminders of Luther's testimony. But I have met some fellow Presbyterians who seem to be out of their element on the fresh water of God's grace. I recall speaking on justification by grace to one of our congregations in a north suburb of Chicago and being challenged by the pastor himself, who asked me: Didn't I realize that I was addressing a congregation in which the majority were highly successful, self-made men? How could I expect them to accept the strange idea that there was one department of their life in which they could not pay their way? He did not mention the rest of the congregation, who perhaps deserved even greater merit for living with self-made men. Anyway, I could only answer him with another question: What did the Savior mean when he said that the strong have no need for the doctor, but only those who are sick (Mark 2:17)?

On another occasion, in a similarly well-to-do Presbyterian church in the city, a man came up to me after I had spoken about the gospel of grace and asked in surprise: "Do you really believe that, or were you just saying it?" I hope he was surprised by grace, and not by any lack of conviction in my voice. Since he shook my hand enthusiastically, I suspect that he, at least, found grace to be a welcome surprise, not an affront to his self-esteem. Grace really does come as a surprise. For as Thomas Aquinas (c. 1225–74) says, the justification of the ungodly, in respect of what it achieves, is a greater work of God than the creation of heaven and earth.

The Presbyterians, if they don't read Thomas or Luther as they should, ought at least to learn from their own reformer, John Calvin (1509–64), that to be justified by grace is to "have in heaven instead of a Judge a gracious Father." Grace—unmerited favor—is a parent's love. Servants, Calvin points out, are afraid to come before their masters until they have finished the day's assignment and have done it right. But children, he continues, will show their parents rough, unfinished, and even spoiled projects, confident that they will find approval anyway. "We need this assurance," Calvin says, "in no slight degree, for without it we attempt everything in vain."

IV

The assurance does not come easily, it seems, to any of us—not even to Luther, who knew from his own experience that faith sometimes has to struggle with the feelings of the heart and to grasp the "Yes" hidden in God's "No" to us. In his advancing years, Luther wondered whether he himself had really trusted the grace of God. The problem is that in the hour of crisis, when disaster strikes or death threatens, the image returns of the Heavenly Judge, who keeps the logbook of our actions and tots them all up. When things go wrong, it isn't easy to remember the Father who pities us children and does not deal with us according to our sins (Ps. 103:10, 13). It is easier to suppose instead that we are being punished, even if we are not certain what we are being punished for. And this leads me to add one last comment on my text.

Paul's desire is this: "If only I may accomplish my course and the ministry which I received from the Lord Jesus, to testify to the gospel of the grace of God." His ministry is a witness not just to grace, but to the *gospel* of grace. What this means comes through more clearly perhaps in the Letter to Titus, where we read that "the grace of God *has appeared*" (Titus 2:11). Paul does not simply recommend grace to us as a fine idea, but announces, rather, that it has been made manifest: grace has come in the person of Jesus of Nazareth, whom the Gospel of John describes as the Word made flesh, full of grace and truth (John 1:14). If, then, we ourselves are out of our element when it comes to God's grace, our help lies in the words and works of the Savior, for whom the grace of God is the very air he breathes.

May God not afflict the church with a famine of the Word, but raise up many more Luthers to testify, with the Apostle Paul, to the gospel of grace. When all is said and done, grace is the deepest truth of our being, and the gospel is the real treasure of the church.

The Call to Worship

"I was glad when they said to me,
'Let us go to the house of the LORD!'"
Psalm 122:1

The joy of worship is something that most of us must have known at one time or another, or we might not be here this morning. The sound of music and the spoken word, the sight of a majestic shrine or a hallowed ritual, have an amazing power to lift our spirits, and we come back hoping for more. Sometimes, even the exhilaration of song does not seem enough to convey our sense of a divine presence; we would gladly throw off the restraints of a genteel life and, like King David, *dance* before the Lord with all our might (2 Sam. 6:14).

Our joy is all the greater if we find ourselves returning to the sanctuary after a time of absence, as the psalmist did. When distance, or some personal pain, or even neglect have kept you away, then going to church is like going back home. It does you good. None of us quite realize, until we're home again, just how much we missed it. And it can be the same with church. Then I'm glad that someone, or some voice within, said to me, "Let us go to the house of the LORD!"

But alas! It isn't always like that. There are those other times, too, when nothing seems to go right in the house of the Lord. I don't like the music; the lessons seem tedious and archaic; the preacher speaks wingless words; and my thoughts take a trip to the Bahamas. By the time I'm back in my house, hungry and unfed, I am not at all glad that I joined the pilgrims in the house of the Lord; I'm saying to myself, "I should have stayed in bed."

Well, it would be strange if churchgoing were totally

different from the rest of life. The pilgrim doesn't fly from mountain peak to mountain peak, but has to go down and cross the valleys. Worshiping is something to work at, like living in general, if we are not to become captive to every accident and every mood. "Liturgy" means "the people's work," or so the linguists say. At any rate, the liturgy takes us through certain actions by which the deeper meaning of our lives is lifted up, acted out, confirmed, and celebrated.

In fact, worship isn't just *like* the rest of life; it *enacts* our life, represents it as it is supposed to be—not simply elevating our mood (though it does that sometimes), but enlightening the mind, and strengthening the will, and capturing the imagination. In this sense, worship stays with us on weekdays. One day in God's courts may be better than a thousand anywhere else, but the blessed are those who dwell in God's house all the days of their life (Pss. 27:4; 84:4, 10).

But by "liturgy" I don't mean (for now) anything quite so elaborate as Dom Gregory Dix had in mind when he wrote his famous book, *The Shape of the Liturgy*. I mean simply what the people do, or work at, when they go into the house of the Lord, or even into a church that styles itself "nonliturgical." I admit that the cultivation of "free" worship does sometimes leave us at the mercy of the pastor's whims and hides the very point of worship.

Recall, for instance, the classic example of free prayer, or what used to be called "conceived prayer," in *Drums along the Mohawk*. To the Rev. Mr. Rosenkranz, prayer brings certain things to God's divine notice, and he ends by bringing things to the notice of his congregation. He begins, "O Almighty God," but provides information the Almighty must have been well acquainted with already: that Mary Wollaber is going with a Massachusetts man and has strayed from the path of virtue; that Joe Bellinger has had eleven couples lambed from his twelve ewes, "which is a record in this county"; that General Burgoyne is leading an army against Ticonderoga, and "it certainly looks like war." And so on. The prayer concludes with the immortal words: "The muster will be at eight o'clock sharp on Monday morning. For Christ's sake. Amen."

As one of the old Puritans said: "I do observe a great deal of conceived prayer which is good, but may do better in the sermon." And a great deal more, we may add, that would do better still in the announcements. Sometimes it is hard for the point of worship to get through. But there are at least three elements of worship that are common to every church, even to those that renounce the constraints of a fixed liturgy. Our psalm contains them all. The call to worship—the invitation to go to the house of the Lord—calls us to an act of recollection, an act of community, and an act of homage. And in every one of these three respects it does not call "time out" from ordinary life, but invites us to view our life more clearly.

I

The psalmist must have lived in the country, at a distance from Jerusalem. It was a rare privilege for him to join one of the pilgrim bands on their way to the Temple. He stands spellbound at the gates of the Holy City, and as he does so he begins to recollect all that the city and the Temple have meant to him. There, in Jerusalem, the thrones of the house of David had been set (v. 5); the Holy City has been, and still is, the center of the religion of Israel, for the house of the Lord is there (v. 9).

Worship, first of all, is *an act of recollection*, of remembering. No doubt, some things are best forgotten, and it is self-destructive to live in the past. The Apostle Paul, "forgetting what lies behind," declares, "I press on" (Phil. 3:13–14). But what he wants to set aside is satisfaction with past achievement, as though no further progress were required. He cannot mean us to forget everything. Only by remembering do we discover who we are, and recollection is simply deliberate remembering. Few things horrify us more than total amnesia, which we rightly see as a tragic loss of self. We go into the house of the Lord not to forget, but to let our memories be well formed.

What we hear and learn in the Lord's house stays with us more than we realize. The child rebels against the burden of memorizing, or endures it by doing the assignment mechanically. But what is learned without reflection may still become the truth of our being. In his poem "Clifton Chapel," Henry Newbolt pictures a proud alumnus showing his son around the school chapel:

> This is the Chapel: here, my son,
> Your father thought the thoughts of youth,
> And heard the words that one by one
> The touch of Life has turned to truth.

I would hope that any son of mine might learn truths in chapel a little less jingoistic than Sir Henry's thoughts of "manhood and the vows of war." But the point is a sound one: for the poet, as for the psalmist, the house of the Lord is a place of memory and recollection, and so a place for discovering who we are.

Another psalmist carries his pain to God in prayer and wonders if it is God who needs to be reminded: "Has God forgotten to be gracious?" (Ps. 77:9). But then he sees that his affliction is his own forgetfulness, and he puts his life back together again by recollection: "I will call to mind the deeds of the LORD;/I will remember your wonders of old" (v. 11). Worship is an act of recollection.

II

Notice that in both the psalms I have quoted recollection is also, and at the same time, the recognition of belonging to a whole company of the faithful. For what is brought to mind is chiefly that one is part of a people with whom God had dealings in the old days, and still does. Second, then, worship is *an act of community*. Jerusalem, with its house of the Lord, is the bond that binds the scattered tribes of Israel together, and it is the place where the demands of God's justice have ruled the community. "There the thrones for judgment were set up,/the thrones of the house of David" (Ps. 122:5). And so the pilgrim thinks of his or her brethren and companions, fellow travelers, and the historic people to which both the pilgrim and they belong. Recollection turns to petition and commitment: the pilgrim prays for the peace and prosperity of the Holy City and resolves to seek its good. The pilgrim discovers himself or herself in the community.

There, surely, is the difference between public worship and private prayer. Though we may pray for the "church" at home, in worship the community is immediately present to us, lending us its support and awakening us to its demands. Burdens borne in solitude may be forgotten in church—long enough for us to recover our senses. A recent psychological study finds that "seasonal affective disorder" (SAD, for short) runs rampant through our college campuses in the winter, filling us with loneliness and self-doubt. If you are clinically depressed, going to church shouldn't be expected to cure you. But worship is a tonic, not least because it takes us out of ourselves and sets us in the company of the "royal priesthood," that company of God's own people who recollect the wonderful deeds of God (1 Peter 2:9).

We live in community: we receive from one another, we intercede for one another. Worship reminds us that this is one of the most fundamental chords of our being, and it always points us beyond the walls of the Holy City to a wider human community for which, in some small way, our little community is responsible.

III

Lastly, worship is *an act of homage*, for the final act of self-discovery is to recognize that the Lord is God: "It is [God] that made us, and not we ourselves" (Ps. 100:3). The tribes go up to Jerusalem, as was decreed, "to give thanks to the name of the LORD" (Ps. 122:4). To worship is a duty, a "decree," an obligation; it is an offering, a sacrifice, an oblation. But what can we offer the Lord of the universe, who says: "If I were hungry, I would not tell you,/for the world and all that is in it is mine" (Ps. 50:12)? And the answer is: "Offer to God a sacrifice of thanksgiving" (v. 14).

Thankfulness is the recognition that what we are is, in the end, something given to us. This may not be an attitude we cultivate very assiduously in a university, which sets great store by individual achievement. And I'm all in favor of that. But even in our highly competitive world, the complementary truth is that every achievement is handing on an inheritance we have received from others. There is no individual discovery, no individual insight, without faithfulness to a sacred trust, and gratitude is therefore not an unreasonable duty.

Here, as always, worship is not a separate department of life. The call to worship summons us to see our life more profoundly. We live in great and goodly cities that we did not build, and in houses full of good things, which we did not fill. That's the way the world is made: it rests on grace. And we are to take heed not to forget it (Deut. 6:10–12).

Just about the best thing I have ever read on the meaning of worship is an eloquent sermon by Martin Luther (1483–1546) on Luke 17:11–19, the story of Jesus and the ten lepers. Ten were healed, but only one turned back and fell at Jesus' feet in gratitude. "This is true worship," Luther comments, "to 'turn back and with a loud voice glorify God.' . . . Oh, how few they are who so turn back— scarce one in ten."

When I was an undergraduate at Cambridge years ago, I liked to ride my bicycle to nearby Ely and visit the grand old cathedral. On one such occasion, a friend and I were wandering around the nave when it came time for evensong, so we sat down quietly in one of the pews, totally alone: we were the whole congregation in that massive sanctuary. From the distant chancel a clergyman spotted us and waved us up to sit with the choir. We sat through an unforgettably beautiful service.

Afterward, I chatted with the amiable clergyman and asked him if he didn't get despondent sometimes that nobody attended the service. He realized that he had a Protestant on his hands and gave me a look of pity. He explained patiently that worship is an "office," a duty owed to God. And though no congregation was visible, since the farmhands were all in the fields, the church bell assured them that on their behalf God was receiving the honor due to God's name.

Well, perhaps a really sharp Protestant might take that as an excuse to lie in bed and listen to the bells. But in fact I have never forgotten that sound lesson in Catholic devotion. It became for me then, and still is in my memory, a part of the call to worship—along with the contagious joy of the psalmist, "I was glad when they said to me,/'Let us go to the house of the LORD!'"

The Promise of Baptism

"The promise is to you and to your children."
Acts 2:39

You must have noticed that in the "Western" movies the local minister is commonly referred to as the "preacher." We ourselves often follow the same custom. We ask, "Who's the preacher at First Church?" But as a matter of fact, when ministers are installed they are commissioned in most Protestant churches "to preach the Word and administer the *sacraments.*" The full title is "minister of the Word and *Sacraments.*" To say just "the preacher" is to select only a part of the job.

Indeed, the "charge" addressed to a newly installed minister makes it clear that he or she is a lot of other things besides: a pastor, or shepherd, to the flock for instance; also (in my denomination, at least) a "presbyter," who acts as a link between the local congregation and other churches in the "presbytery." But, so far as our Sunday services of worship are concerned, the most obvious duties of the minister are these two: to preach the Word of God and to perform the two ceremonies, Baptism and the Lord's Supper, to which we give the mystifying name of "sacraments." One of the most important tasks a minister has is to explain what is supposed to be going on when one or the other of these two sacraments is being performed.

In some ways, it's not a very easy task to explain the meaning of Baptism and the Lord's Supper. For one thing, they both have behind them some two thousand years of history, during which a great variety of different meanings have been found in them. And, like everything else that we do very often, we may find ourselves taking

the sacraments for granted, pretty much as a child un-
thinkingly salutes the flag before classes begin at school.
It's simply part of the ritual.

Perhaps we could say that the Lord's Supper, at least,
needs very little explanation. There's the table, and on
Communion Sundays it is covered with a tablecloth on
which are placed bread and wine. Obviously, it's a meal:
we are sitting down to eat and drink together. It's not an
ordinary meal, of course. It is designed to remind us that
our bodies are not the only part of us that needs nourishment. There's more to us than arms, legs, a head, and so
forth; there is also that strange something we call the
"soul." And our souls too need to be fed. We all know
what it is to be hungry. But there is a hunger that three
meals a day cannot satisfy, a hunger of the soul.

And the food of the soul is the One who said: "I am the
bread of life. Whoever comes to me will never be hungry,
and whoever believes in me will never be thirsty" (John
6:35). In some mysterious way (which none of us ever fully
understands), it is as we look to Jesus the Christ that our
other hunger is satisfied.

> Bread of the world in mercy broken,
> Wine of the soul in mercy shed,
> . . . .
> Be thy feast to us the token
> That by thy grace our souls are fed.

That is what the Lord's Supper means—or, at least,
that's its most obvious meaning. I certainly don't want to
deny that the Lord's Supper means a good many things,
fully enough to keep ministers provided with sermon topics for the rest of their lives. But the chief significance
Communion Sunday has for us is this: In the breaking of
the bread our Lord calls to our minds that he alone is the
food of our souls and that we may seek satisfaction for our
spiritual hunger solely in him. And that's a point we can
hardly miss as we see the table laid ready for us and hear
the invitation given in Christ's name by the minister.

But how about the sacrament of Baptism? Is there a
similarly obvious meaning for this other ceremony?

Whatever can be the point of sprinkling water on the head of a newborn babe?

Here too the main point seems fairly clear. Just as bread nourishes our bodies, so water cleans them. The Lord's Supper tells us that our souls need food and nourishment just as much as our bodies; and baptism reminds us that the soul, like the body, needs cleansing. If we cannot live in this world without getting hungry, neither can we go about our daily business without getting our hands dirty. Baptism tells us that the cleansing of our souls, as well as their sustenance, comes from the same Jesus Christ. This is what Ananias meant when he said to Paul: "Get up, be baptized, and have your sins washed away, calling on his name" (Acts 22:16). Or, as one of the old catechisms puts it: "The forgiveness of sins is a kind of washing, by which our souls are cleansed from their defilements, just as the stains of the body are washed away by water."

So far, so good: it looks as though baptism too, like the Lord's Supper, has a very simple meaning. But *washing* is not its only meaning. There is also scriptural warrant for saying that baptism is a kind of *drowning* of the old, sinful self. (See Rom. 6:4; Col. 2:12.) And, on reflection, even the notion of washing seems problematic. The difficulty is that many Christians have spoken as if the actual pouring of the water on the infant's forehead itself cleansed the child from all sins. I have heard a mother say after a baptismal service: "Now he's a Christian—he'll go to heaven." And I daresay you have heard much the same thing said. While we fully sympathize with the high opinion of baptism that such a belief implies, we may doubt that the mere pouring of water on a child's brow could of itself make a disciple of Christ, or that the neglect of it could send a child to hellfire. Christians have debated whether it is right to say that "regeneration" or "the new birth" actually happens at the precise moment when baptism is administered; *some* Christians have argued it is wrong to baptize infants at all. Washing a soul is not really quite so simple as washing your hands before lunch—even though the hand-washing serves as a sort of figure or illustration of what happens when God removes the stains of sin from our lives.

What, then, does the child receive in baptism? Perhaps we can agree on this much: that the child receives the *promise* of cleansing. This is really the only point I want to make this morning. Whatever more each of us may wish to say, baptism is the promise of cleansing. It is God's way of telling us what God's plans are for the child. To make God's intentions quite clear, God doesn't merely *tell*, God *shows* us. And we are invited to share in the plans, which demand that we too make certain promises. Actually, three promises are made in baptism: one by the parents, one by the congregation, and one (the most important) by God.

I

First, a promise is made by the parents. They are asked to give assurance that they will bring up their child in the "nurture and admonition of the Lord." In other words, in our service of baptism we declare our belief in the enormous power for good that can be exercised by a truly Christian home. A child's sense of values and picture of God are largely taken from the parents—and they are taken more from what the parents do than from what they say. In a sense, to Christian parents is committed the task of creating a new soul.

A high opinion of the Christian home is something Christian people have always held to. But in our own day we should be glad to find that the psychologists (those high priests of our twentieth-century American society) are saying much the same thing. Present-day psychology has placed tremendous emphasis on what it calls "the formative years of childhood." The mind of the child, as Carl Jung (1875–1961), one of the most distinguished of European psychoanalysts, put it, is as "soft and pliable as wax." And he insists that impressions are made on this tablet of wax not merely by "good and pious precepts," but by what he describes as the "peculiarly affective state"—the emotional atmosphere, let's say—in which the family lives. Quite unconsciously, the child breathes in this atmosphere, and it can be spiritually poisonous or healthy. How crucial it is, then, that this intangible "atmosphere" should be permeated by the parents' firm faith in Jesus Christ.

No parents can force their children to become Christians; sooner or later each of us has to make a decision. But what the parents can do is well illustrated by the story of one lad whose mother prayed for him for over thirty years. Despite the benefits of a Christian education, the youth turned against his mother's faith and caused her fearful grief by living with a woman who was not his wife. But the mother kept praying, long after most of us would have given up, perhaps with a few bitter remarks about the ingratitude of the younger generation. Finally, when the young man was thirty-two years old, his mother's prayers were answered: He became a Christian. And what a Christian! Saint Augustine (he's the one I have in mind) became the most influential thinker, next to Paul, that the Western church has ever known.

Long ago one of our Puritan forefathers made the astute remark that the family is "the seminary of Church and State." And he added:

> Doubtless many an excellent magistrate hath been sent into the Commonwealth, and many an excellent pastor into the Church, and many a precious saint to heaven, through the happy preparations of a holy education— perhaps by a woman that thought herself useless and unserviceable to the Church.

If it were so more often, he remarks, then one pastor would not have to do the work of two or three hundred parents!

II

Second, in the service of baptism a promise is made by the whole congregation. The congregation is called on to promise that, with God's help, they will do all within their power to bring the child to the day when he or she will confess Jesus Christ as Lord and Savior. In some service books the congregation is required to say "We do so promise," just as the parents are required to answer "I do" to the questions put to them.

Much the same things that were said of the parents apply here too. Indeed, what is a Christian congregation but an extension of the Christian family? In receiving a child for baptism, the congregation accepts the responsibility for seeing that he or she will be given a Christian education in the church school. Perhaps even more important, each of us accepts the responsibility of showing the child, by the way we talk and behave, what it is to be a Christian. It is really quite sobering to realize to what a large extent our children's treatment by a Sunday school teacher, or by the person sitting next to them in the pew, or by the minister, the choir director, or anyone else, may form their image of what it means to be a disciple of Christ.

III

Baptism is the making of a promise by the parents, by the congregation, and, third (and most important), by God. For if the child finally grows to Christian maturity, as we hope and expect, then neither the parents nor the congregation dare take the credit: they are no more than the agents through whom God brings the divine purpose to completion. One may sow the seed, and another may give it water—but God gives the increase, makes the seed to grow (1 Cor. 3:7). God's plan is to sanctify the life of the child through the ministry of home and church. Without *God's* promise, nothing else could be of any use.

That God makes this promise even to a helpless infant is a most eloquent testimony to the way in which God deals with humanity. When we were brought to the waters of baptism, we were quite unable to contribute anything to the ceremony—except perhaps a little mild resistance. We knew nothing of what God was doing, and had done, on our behalf. How better could one picture a gracious God who in Christ did something for me without ever consulting me or waiting for my approval? It is never God's way to wait for us to make the first move. No matter how early we get up in the morning, the grace of God has been at work before us. God loved us before we loved God, before we ever knew God or could know God. "We love," says John, "because he first loved us" (1 John 4:19). That is the meaning of God's promise in our baptism.

Here, then, in this sacrament we have nothing less than the gospel itself impressed on us in a striking and vivid way: I contribute no more to my salvation than an infant contributes to baptism. I am called to "work out" my salvation, but even this is the work of God in me (Phil. 2:12–13). True, the same point could be made in a sermon without baptism. But one of the most important things about sermons is that they're easily forgotten! Especially do we forget them when we most need them—that is, when we are going through a period of severe temptation, when we are on the verge of despairing about this whole business called "Christianity." When Martin Luther (1483–1546) was tormented by such doubts (as even the most devout of believers is at some time or other), he would take a piece of chalk and write on his desk, "I have been baptized." He didn't mean that this made him a Christian. He meant that in his baptism there was one sermon he could never forget—even if he remembered nothing about it! God had promised. This was the one constant thing on which he felt he could rely. Throughout all our changing moods and distressing doubts, God remains true to God's Word. If God showed care for us before we ever came to have faith, God still cares even when the faith we now have begins to waver.

The trouble lies, not in the uncertainty of our baptism, but in the fact that we don't *use* our baptism. One of the questions in "The Westminster Larger Catechism" asks, "How is our Baptism to be improved [that is, used] by us?" And the answer is: "The needful but much neglected duty of improving our Baptism, is to be performed by us all our life long, especially in time of temptation, and when we are present at the administration of it to others." In other words, that unspoken sermon preached to us in our infancy, when we did not understand it, is preached to us again and again each time we witness the baptism of another. May God give each one of us the grace to use that sermon faithfully. The promise is to us—and to our children.

Remembrance of Things Present

"Do this in remembrance of me."
1 Corinthians 11:24–25

In Paul's account of the Last Supper, these are the words with which the Lord offers first the bread, then the cup, to his disciples. He took a loaf, gave thanks, broke it, and said: "This is my body that is for you. Do this in remembrance of me." Then he took the cup, when they had eaten, and said: "This cup is the new covenant in my blood. Do this, as often as you drink it, in remembrance of me."

We will hear the familiar words in our service of worship when we celebrate Communion; and they will be a bond of unity with millions of fellow Christians, of every color and race, in every corner of the globe, who, like ourselves, will be following the Savior's bidding. In Paul's vivid metaphor: "Because there is one loaf, we, many as we are, are one body; for it is one loaf of which we all partake" (1 Cor. 10:17, New English Bible).

"Do this in remembrance of me." For almost two thousand years, and in almost every Christian community, the Lord's mandate has placed at the heart of Christian worship what the Apostle calls "the Lord's supper" (11:20). Others have called it "the Eucharist," "the Mass," "the Sacrament of the Altar," "the breaking of Bread," "the Holy Communion." For all the differences of ceremony and meaning that these diverse names suggest, the words that authorize the rite are everywhere the same—translated into many languages. Few things can give Christians a more exhilarating sense of the great company of saints, living and dead, that has gratefully received the bread of life from Nazareth, and still does. Augustine described the Lord's Supper as "the bond of love," and the Council of Trent called it "this sign of unity . . . this symbol of concord."

But the sad truth is that these descriptions have a bitter, ironic ring to them. The several strands in the New Testament's statements about the Lord's Supper have come unraveled, and sharp disagreement over the meaning of the central Christian rite has set Christian against Christian, theologian against theologian, church against church. Devout believers have gone to the stake and been burned because, among other things, they held unacceptable views on this "sign of unity," this "symbol of concord." So acrimonious did the conflict become at the time of the Reformation that one theologian (Kaspar Schwenkfeld; 1489–1561) called for a temporary suspension of the rite, pending a better understanding of it. Others gave it up altogether as a merely outward and earthly symbol of an inward and spiritual communion with Christ, which could better be had without it.

Even in our own day, when we applaud the ecumenical movement in the church, Christians exclude one another from the Lord's Table for holding a different understanding of it. It is pointless for those who want "open Communion" to be censorious of their brothers and sisters who do not and who, in good conscience, cannot. We can only mourn a little together, think further together, and be thankful that the sign of unity, though terribly damaged by our divisions, has not quite been severed.

"Do this in remembrance of me." Is it still possible to use these words for edification, and not to start an argument? I hope so, and I'll try. It is a short enough text, and each part of it is equally important.

I

"*Do this.*" The words "Do this" transform Jesus' last meal with his disciples into a perpetual observance of the church—a "sacrament," as most but not all of us say. Protestants have sometimes asked, much to the disapproval

of the Catholics: Why do we need the Sacrament if salvation is by faith, and if faith comes by hearing the Word
(Rom. 10:17)? Didn't Paul himself say that Christ sent him
to preach the gospel, that God, in God's wisdom, was
pleased to save those who believe through the foolishness
of preaching (1 Cor. 1:17, 21)? Why the Sacrament too?

Well, unfortunately, we aren't all as good at preaching
the gospel as Paul must have been. Our sermons are
sometimes foolish for the wrong reasons. A Catholic
friend of mine said after attending a Protestant service of
worship: "That was awful. It was like listening to another
lecture." She was already signed up for six hours of lecture
a week, and she looked for something else when she went
to church.

My own persuasion is that there is a very important difference between a lecture and a sermon. A lecture is supposed to contribute to that increase of knowledge to
which the university is dedicated. *Crescat scientia!* ("Let
knowledge increase [that life may flourish].") The sermon, on the other hand, is to increase our commitment to
some things that we know, for the most part, already. If
this is a lecture I'm giving, I'm afraid it isn't a very good
one. As usual, I quietly sidestep many of the fascinating
questions we love to talk about in class.

No, a sermon is not a lecture. Still, even good preaching, if we could manage it, wouldn't make it wise to dis-
pense with the Sacrament. We are to *do*, as well as to *speak*.
There is, in fact, a directness and forcefulness in the simple actions and formulas of the Eucharist that can sometimes lift the spirits even of a word-weary Protestant, well
able to sympathize with a Catholic friend. But to set word
and sign over against each other is a mistake, if the purpose of both is to renew our commitment to the light and
life that have come into our world through Jesus Christ.
Each needs the other.

Christian preachers do not have unlimited freedom to
talk about whatever they please. It is not enough even to
say that they are bound by their text. They speak, like the
Apostle, as servants of Christ (Rom. 1:1; Gal. 1:10), and
the sacrament of Christ's body and blood holds them to

their task. Martin Luther (1483–1546) certainly wished
the sermon to correct false understandings of the Sacrament, but he well understood the power of the Sacrament
to direct the content of the sermon. "Our popular sermons," he wrote, "ought to be nothing else than exposi-
tions of the mass." Why? Because it is in the Mass, as
Luther here calls it, that Christian faith is properly focused. Which brings me to the second part of my text.

II

"Do this *in remembrance*." To grasp the point of these
words, we might recast them in the negative, and read:
"Do this, so that you do not forget." This is the only
express reason the Lord gives for the institution of the
Sacrament in the church: it is a reminder, lest we forget.
And Paul's addition in verse 26 says much the same thing:
"For as often as you eat this bread and drink the cup, you
proclaim the Lord's death until he comes" (1 Cor. 11:26).
The Sacrament is itself a kind of proclamation, or preaching—a visible word, a sermon addressed to the congregation, not in spoken words but in actions. As such, it is a
constant reminder to Christians not to forget that they are
who they are and what they are because the Lord has
given them the new covenant in his blood (v. 25).

Christian tradition has always understood the Lord's
Supper as the church's equivalent of the Hebrew
Passover, the "day of remembrance" (Ex. 12:14), of which
we read in the Old Testament lesson. The purpose of the
Hebrew observance was to be a perpetual reminder of the
deliverance from Egypt: "so that all the days of your life
you may remember the day of your departure from the
land of Egypt" (Deut. 16:3). Remembrance, similarly, is
the purpose of the Lord's Supper. "For even Christ our
passover is sacrificed for us" (1 Cor. 5:7, KJV).

We shouldn't overlook the fact that Paul had a special
reason for introducing the Christian reminder where he
does. The setting gives it a meaning that is as pertinent to
our situation as it was to the situation of the church at
Corinth. The church was split into factions, each rallying

around its own party leader. Competition and quarreling between the cliques were tearing the church apart (1 Cor. 3:3–5). This was the main problem that led Paul to send the Corinthian Christians this letter. The Corinthians divided into their cliques even when they gathered together to celebrate the Supper of the Lord. "What I mean," he writes, "is that each of you says, 'I belong to Paul,' or 'I belong to Apollos,' or 'I belong to Cephas [Peter]'" (1:12). Some said (apparently), "I belong to Christ" (1:12).

Paul has already admonished them that it was Christ, not Paul (or anyone else), who was crucified for them, and Christ is not divided. We dare not even say our allegiance is to Christ if we say it to justify separation from other Christians. In this setting, the sacramental reminder of the Lord's Supper takes on a particular force. "Do this in remembrance of me" means: "Do not forget the only one who can rightfully claim your allegiance."

Sociologist Robert Wuthnow has said that, in our own day, the churches have largely become holding companies for special interest groups. A disturbing thought, but only too true! So many causes compete for our allegiance—good causes, many of them—that they threaten to divide us. The Sacrament calls us back to the center, when we forget. Christian memories are at least as short as Jewish memories. We all need our days of remembrance.

III

The trouble is, however, that the very word "remembrance" is sometimes taken to imply a view of the Lord's Supper that deeply offends the great majority of Christians. One commentator expressly points out that it is always an *absent* friend that we "remember." Another infers, more bluntly: "There is no magic, no mystery, no 'sacrament' about it. . . . And away goes the whole fabric of superstitious Christianity." Even Luther once described the Lord's Supper as Christ's "requiem"—a memorial to the departed Christ. Remembering seems to imply an event gone by, a person no longer with us. And that doesn't sound right to most of us.

Far be it from me to take up the cause of "superstitious Christianity"! We all know that talk of a "real presence" in the Eucharist led to those medieval legends about bleeding wafers in the priest's hands, and the like. Superstitious legends they may be, and we can understand the warning one contemporary of Luther gave: If anyone says to you, "Christ is here [in the bread]," don't believe it (cf. Matt. 24:2). And yet, behind the legends lies the sound conviction that it is impossible for Christians to think of their Lord as simply "the departed." And, actually, that is not what the critics of the real presence ever wanted to say.

The text says, not "Do this to commemorate my death," but: "Do this in remembrance of me." *Of me!* That's my third point. For Paul, and for Christians ever since, the text can only mean: Remember the living Lord, who is not absent but remains faithful to his promise to be with you always, to the end of the world (Matt. 28:20).

One of John Calvin's (1509–64) fellow Reformers, Heinrich Bullinger (1504–75), took his stand firmly on the idea of remembrance, which, to him, ruled out any talk of a real presence in the Sacrament. Calvin wrote him a letter in reply, in which he explained: "*I* say that in the Lord's Supper there is a remembrance of something present." A "remembrance of *something present*"! To my mind, that is exactly right. The Sacrament is not only a memorial of Christ's death (though it surely is that): it is a remembrance of the gift and demand of the ever-present Lord, whose claim on his disciples they so easily forget. Through the bread and wine he gives himself to them again and again, and they, in return, give themselves to him, acknowledging his right to their devotion.

But so habitual is our association of remembrance with absence that somewhere between my reflections on the Sacrament and the announcement of my topic for this sermon the title was changed from "Remembrance of Things Present" to "Remembrance of Things Past." I confidently concluded that the editor of my announcement must be more at home in Shakespeare or Marcel Proust than in Calvin. But I really did say "Remembrance of Things Present," and (with acknowledgments to Calvin) I meant it.

The Anglican reformer Thomas Cranmer (1489–1556) put it well in this confession made at his trial: "I believe, that whoso eateth and drinketh that sacrament, Christ is within them, whole Christ, his nativity, passion, resurrection, and ascension." Alas, he was burned at the stake anyway. Perhaps it was politics. In our more generous ecumenical world, we can come to the Sacrament with something like Cranmer's confession, and can leave it to our theology lectures to explain how it happens.

Do this in remembrance of things always present, but still forgotten.

Pilgrims

The Immigrants

"How shall we sing the LORD's song
in a strange land?"
Psalm 137:4
"We are citizens of Heaven."
Philippians 3:20

"The Immigrants." I hardly need to tell you that I am one of them; my speech betrays me, like Peter's in the Gospel story (Matt. 26:73). I have a personal interest in the subject, and my eye was irresistibly drawn to a report on New York immigrants in a recent newspaper column. I learned that there are good things and bad things to say about resident aliens. Mentioned first on the good side was this: "Aliens fill jobs that no one else wanted." I found that reassuring. No one else really wanted the job I took. I hope nobody does now.

On the debit side, the first item on the list was this: "Some aliens resist learning English." That troubled me. But I assume a regular exception is made for English aliens, like myself, who have learned the language fairly well after their fashion. I was also unconvinced by disadvantage four: immigrants "cause culture shock for older residents."

The truth is, of course, that we immigrants are a very assorted bunch. This was brought home to me, as never before, when I received my U.S. citizenship. After the official swearing-in, the new citizens were invited to a follow-up meeting in the Methodist Chicago Temple. I didn't know what to expect. But I was surprised when I was handed a bulletin at the door that resembled in detail an order of worship. There was a prelude on the piano, an invocation, a pledge of allegiance (a recital of the creed, you might say). There were musical selections. (The ancient Roman Pliny [62–113 C.E.], if he could have been there, would have noticed that we sang hymns to America *quasi deo*, as if to a deity.) There were many good words from the rostrum. And, finally, there was a receiving line, in which we were presented with little flags to place on our desks or bedside tables.

I

Some of my colleagues have written books about civil religion; I felt that I had personally been there. My thoughts went back to a lecture I heard in New York many years ago by the distinguished British philosopher Dorothy Emmet (b. 1904). She told us that on the journey over on the ocean liner *Queen Elizabeth* (it really was a long time ago), she had attended a very British worship service. The altar was draped with a Union Jack; a huge portrait of the Queen looked down on the worshipers; and the captain prayed at length and in detail for the nation and the several members of the royal family. Seeing that some of us were shocked, Miss Emmet said: "I rather liked it."

And so did I on my citizenship day. What was burned most indelibly into my memory was the time set aside for what I can only call the "personal testimonies." As it happened, I had come in among the stragglers and had been obliged to sit prominently in the front row. At the point on the bulletin where it said "Responses by New Citizens," the delightful and charming lady who presided over the meeting beckoned me up to the platform. That was a mistake. The stereotype of the reserved Englishman was actually made to describe me. And when she asked me what was in my heart on this momentous occasion, I couldn't find anything there worth sharing. Pressed to say at least if I wasn't glad to be a citizen, I agreed that I was. Then I was sent back to my seat in disgrace.

The next testimony was totally different. A young woman rose to her feet and, with tears streaming down her face, told how she had escaped from a country where many of her relatives were literally held prisoner. And, one after another, a host of similar testimonies followed. Only the limits of time called the fascinating stories to a halt.

I had come from a land of secure democratic institutions to the land of opportunity, and was properly grateful. *They* had come to the land of liberty, some perhaps because they were on the hit list of some death squad, and their emotions overflowed. I chose to be an American citizen because I don't believe in taxation without representation. They chose because the United States had given them—quite literally—new life. I had faithfully done my preparation for citizenship; but now, for the first time, I understood, and I felt a little ashamed of my own cool performance.

II

Even the most ecstatic of immigrants may pay a price, however. The human roots are eroded, perhaps severed. And many an alien must have asked: Where, now, do I really belong? Alistair Cooke (b. 1908) says: "I seem to be perceived in America as a benign old English gentleman, and in England as an enlightened American." Either one, I suppose, is not such a bad thing to be; perhaps Alistair Cooke should be glad to be thought both. But the problem for many immigrants lies in the constant oscillation between *two* identities, and the resulting loss of *clear* identity.

In Ingmar Bergman's saga *The Immigrants*, the wife dies in Minnesota dreaming of home—Sweden. And if I remember rightly, there is a poignant scene in which the bereaved husband stands totally alone outside the house listening to the laughter of his children inside, who are not immigrants but Americans of Swedish descent.

In a little town on Long Island, where I once served a summer pastorate, I met a retired English couple who had lived in America for thirty or forty years but still clung resolutely to their British passports. Maybe my presence stirred uncharacteristic thoughts in them. But they complained about everything, including the fact that the

milkman opened the kitchen door to put the milk inside—
which an English milkman would never do without
knocking.

I have spoken with a cultivated, well-traveled German
lady in Chicago who moved her account to another bank
because a teller called her by her first name—and didn't
pronounce it quite right either.

I don't know how grave these offenses against old-
world courtesies will strike you as being. For now, I am
interested not in the sins but in the symptoms—the breaking out of the hidden, disturbing question: I'm really not
home, am I? Perhaps it will be all right if I work here but
go back to retire there, die there, be buried there. Where
is the motherland, the fatherland, home?

"Home," said the great scholar Erasmus (c. 1466–
1536), "is where my books are." And what scholar can't
say amen to that?

In the town hall in Göttingen, Germany, you can read
the motto: *Ubi bene, ibi patria* ("Where things go well for
me, there is my homeland").

A motto on the portrait of a Swiss Protestant comes
closer to the truth: *Ubi deus meus, ibi patria mea* ("Where
my God is, there is my homeland"). For a patriotic Swiss,
a powerful testimony!

Wearied from the Great War, in which he had seen the
spirit of his nation broken and had buried some of his
nearest and dearest, Ernst Troeltsch (1865–1923) wrote
from Germany to his friend Friedrich von Hügel
(1852–1925) in England: "Man, thank God, possesses a
second Fatherland from which no one can cast him out.
In this other country we are both of us at home."

That surely is it! *Where the kingdom of God is, there is our
country.* And where is that? Everywhere, of course. When
will it come? It has come, and it comes every day.

III

"You are no longer strangers and aliens, but you are citizens with the saints and also members of the household
of God" (Eph. 2:19). That means, to begin with, that in

Jesus Christ we are no longer aliens from the commonwealth of Israel (v. 12). We've been naturalized. But it
does not mean the victorious Israel that put the Canaan-
ites to the sword (Deut. 7:1–6), nor the vanquished Israel
that pined in exile for Zion (Ps. 137). It means an Israel
that has learned, through suffering, its mission to be the
light of the world; and it is a mission that has little to do
with the geography of Palestine (Isa. 42:6; 53:11). The
New Jerusalem is not made with human hands; the better
country, the long-sought homeland, is a heavenly one
(Heb. 11:10, 14, 16). It isn't there rather than here, or
here more than there.

"How shall we sing the LORD's song in a strange land?"
That question, to be sure, did assume that home is back
there, left behind. And there is nothing to do but to weep
and to hang up the harp. The taunt of the captors, "Sing
us one of the songs of Zion!" (Ps. 137:3), must be endured
in grim silence, and the exiles are left with only their
memories of Jerusalem.

"How shall we sing the LORD's song in a strange land?"
There can be few, if any, more moving expressions of the
resident alien's homesickness. One marvels at its simple
poetic perfection. But because it comes from a strictly ge-
ographical patriotism, the beautiful lament passes over
into an ugly curse: "Happy shall they be who pay you back
what you have done to us! Happy shall they be who take
your little ones and dash them against the rock!" (vv. 8–9).
Hate and revenge become the only solace; and patriotism
is still power over other people—only now it is power
anticipated, not yet enjoyed. As terrible a passage as we
could find anywhere in Scripture! But, like everything else
in Scripture, profitable for our instruction and correction
(2 Tim. 3:16). It is into a wiser Israel, chastened by history, that we have been, as Paul puts it, "grafted" (Rom.
11:17–24).

"We are citizens of Heaven" (Phil. 3:20, see Notes). Or,
as another translation has it, "Our citizenship is in heaven"
(NRSV). Or, in yet another version: "We are a colony of
heaven." Perhaps that makes the point best—as citizens of
heaven, fellow citizens with the saints, we remain residents

of the world. We have, if you like, a dual citizenship. And therein lie a lot of our confusions. The best commentary I know on my second text comes from an anonymous Christian apologist of the second century:

> Christians cannot be distinguished from the rest of the human race by country or language or customs. . . . They live in their own countries, but only as aliens. They have a share in everything as citizens, and endure everything as foreigners. Every foreign land is their fatherland, and yet for them every fatherland is a foreign land. . . . To put it simply: What the soul is in the body, that Christians are in the world. The soul is dispersed through all the members of the body, and Christians are scattered through all the cities of the world. . . . [Christians] hold the world together.

IV

Would that it were so! There is a touch of presumption in those last words—if we take them as a description, not a challenge; as a journalist's report, and not an immensely powerful idea that we need more desperately today than ever.

The Christian vision of a global community can as easily be tarnished as the American ideal of a great multiracial homeland. As the columnist Mike Royko once pointed out in his inimitable style, the European immigrants to Chicago brought all their old prejudices in their tote bags and quickly picked up some new ones, discovering other ethnic groups to hate that they hadn't had to live with before. Not my style, but I suppose there's a lot in that: some things never did dissolve in that great melting pot which might have been, and still might be, an image of the kingdom of God.

But the church isn't doing much better as long as a Christian militia fights Muslims in the Middle East, or Catholics and Protestants mow down their brothers, sisters, and children in Christ in Northern Ireland. And there is a more subtle irony in the fact that we sing "Glorious things of thee are spoken, Zion, city of our God" to the tune for "*Deutschland, Deutschland über alles*"—a universalistic hymn set to a very particularistic European song. Anyone from the old colonial world could suggest a hidden symbolism in that. Keep it in mind next time you sing of Zion.

Not the church, not Christians, but the kingdom of God "holds the world together." The church, by God's sovereign grace, may be a sign and instrument of the kingdom. But it often isn't. And the difficult art of being a Christian has a great deal to do with grasping just such ambiguities of our continuing immigrant status in the world—with its strangely mixed feelings and divided loyalties. Perhaps the immigrant never quite sorts them all out. But when, as Christian immigrants, we pray, "Thy kingdom come," we are saying at least these two things, which may be paradoxical but are not unclear: We are at home everywhere, and we are at home nowhere.

It doesn't matter where we are from, or where we are, or even who or what we are: we recognize one another as fellow citizens, purely by the grace of Christ, in one great commonwealth of heaven. We are home. . . . And yet, wherever we are, we cannot be so comfortably at home in the world that we seek our treasure, and our final security, anywhere else but in the kingdom of God and God's justice (Matt. 6:33).

"How shall we sing the LORD's song in a strange land?"

Answer: "Sing it as 'citizens of Heaven,' and there *is* no strange land—though no land is really home."

Strangers on Earth

*"I am a stranger on the earth:
hide not thy commandments from me."*
Psalm 119:19

I have repeated those words to myself many times over. To me, they have a kind of pathos about them, a plaintive and haunting quality, hard to forget. They are, I think, a profound statement of our human condition; and, like so many cries from the depths, they may have a meaning larger than their author intended.

"I am a stranger on the earth." The psalmist lives in the world like an alien, and he cannot feel himself quite at home in it. He does not really *belong* here, but only *visits*. The house and the country belong to another. And, with the uncertainty of a stranger, he reaches out for guidance. The word "stranger" (or "sojourner") implies only a short visit: he is God's guest for a day, until (as another psalm puts it) he must "go hence, and be no more" (Ps. 39:13). And that makes his cry all the more urgent. His soul is "broken" ("consumed") with longing for some directive from the Lord—a word that may give him his bearing, show him how to conduct himself on his brief visit. If God should withhold this word, conceal from him the rules of the house and the laws of the land, his bewilderment would be more than he could bear. "Hide not thy commandments from me."

A very moving expression of human uncertainty! Yes, but isn't it completely out of tune with the way *modern* humanity experiences the world? Is it perhaps only the professional misfits, like ministers of the Word, who can still resonate today with the age-old cry of the psalmist?

I

Modern men and women, it may be said, do not think of themselves as confused and disoriented in the world, but as masters over it, every year extending their control over the forces of nature. Early humans may have been intimidated by the world, because they imagined that behind every rock and every tree there lurked an assortment of powerful and temperamental demons, ready at any moment to leap out and take them. But for us moderns, the world is there to be manipulated for our own ends, and we need only to learn the principles that make it tick. The demons have been long gone. We have split the atom, harnessed the resources of our planet, and—like Alexander dreaming of new worlds to conquer—we have ventured out into space to explore other, larger worlds. What sense can it possibly make, in the age of sputnik and Skylab, for us to sit here and meditate on the psalmist's ancient cry of lostness?

Well, the truth is that our venture into space has two sides to it. As an immense technical triumph, we can only marvel at it. But it has taught us, besides, just how much more there is to be conquered. And what we proudly call "the conquest of space" is, in fact, merely testing the ocean with the tip of our toe.

Some of you will remember that in 1973 we celebrated, not only Skylab, but the five hundredth birthday of the man who, in a way, made Skylab possible: the Polish cleric and scientist, Nicholaus Copernicus (1473–1543), who opened up our venture into space. At the University of Chicago, a special birthday cake was baked for Copernicus, each layer of the cake representing the orbit of one of the sun's satellites. A guest remarked that Chicago was probably the only place where Copernicus's five hundredth birthday party was celebrated in quite this way. I'm sure he was right.

But when Copernicus's discoveries were first made known, the celebrating was by no means universal. The first printing of his famous book *On the Revolutions of the*

Heavenly Bodies (1543) was brought to him on his deathbed. The author himself lay beyond the reach of any harassment. But the Roman Church later put his treatise on the index of forbidden books; and some say the Protestants would have done the same with it if they'd had their own list of forbidden books. Copernicus had upset Christendom's sacred topography, in which our own planet was the fixed center of the universe, and the universe itself had been fashioned by God for our benefit. If the earth was only a satellite circling the sun, then we were dislocated from the center of things, and for centuries the church had been wrong. Small wonder, really, that Copernicus's book was banned (though he had prudently dedicated it to the pope); or that one of his followers, Giordano Bruno (1548–1600), was relentlessly hounded until he wearily recanted and promised not to tell what he saw when looking through his telescope!

And yet what Copernicus began was only a very small beginning. Since him the universe he opened to our exploration has grown beyond his wildest dreams; and the astronomers today dazzle and dizzy us with statistics that defy the imagination. You remember how, in grade school, the teacher would try to scale things down for us: If the earth were a Ping-Pong ball, it would be a five- or six-minute walk to the sun, and Neptune would be nine miles away—and so on. But a teacher could give us no more than our own solar system with its nine little satellites. Now, I was a classics major, so I may be a few million off. But I think we are told there are over 100 billion stars in the galaxy to which our sun belongs; and there may be as many galaxies as there are stars in the Milky Way. . . . How do you scale *that* down? The mind simply reaches the end of its tether. As Blaise Pascal (1623–62) exclaimed: "What is a man in the infinite? . . . The eternal silence of these infinite spaces frightens me."

For myself, I am not surprised that the church of a bygone age did not like what it saw when Copernicus lifted up a corner of the cosmic veil. Humanity began to lose its bearings in the universe: that is the price we had to pay for the advance of our control over nature. We discovered that we are not the center of things; and that, so far as could be observed, the universe has no center. And then we had to learn from the geologists that the entire history of humankind on the earth has been only a fleeting moment in the four and one-half billion years for which the earth has existed. Neither is there any solid reason to believe that there is life anywhere else in the immense silence of space. What, indeed, is a man (or a woman!) in the infinite?

"I am a stranger on the earth." So far from being an incomprehensible cry from a remote past, the psalmist's words seem, on reflection, a curiously apt expression of what we know today about our place in the mysterious universe, with its unimaginable expanses of space and time. But just how seriously, in practice, do we absorb in our hearts what we know with the tops of our heads?

II

Nowadays, we do not impose silence on our astronomers and geologists, or burn them at the stake. But I wonder how successful we are in adopting their picture of the world into our daily habits of thought or into our estimate of ourselves and our existence. It fascinates us, perhaps disturbs us, and then simply eludes us.

Will you permit me a very homely illustration? When my children were younger, I once sat with them through an episode of the television serial Lost in Space. I daresay my attention was a bit fitful: I really wanted to read the newspaper. But as nearly as I could gather, not being one of the regular viewers (I really prefer Star Trek), a spaceship from the good planet Earth had gone off course; it was stranded in some unknown corner of the heavens and was unable to return home. Of course, I was thinking deep theological thoughts as I watched with half an eye. And it occurred to me that, like so much of our science fiction, Lost in Space conceals the scientific truth from us: it assumes one gets lost in space by leaving Mother Earth and losing one's way, and everything will be fine if only we can get back home again. The immensity of space is there, but the earth is still securely at the center.

With far profounder insight, Pascal recognized that it is we at home on the earth who are lost in space, "lost in this remote corner of nature." In science fiction, strangers on the earth are those green midgets from outer space, most likely from Mars; in hard reality, they are men and women walking their own native soil—with illusions of grandeur, imaging themselves at the center of things.

Anyone who supposes that the Bible is only interested in sin and holiness may be surprised by that other marvelous psalm which we read as our Old Testament lesson (Psalm 8): its theme is so clearly humanity in space, not humanity in sin.

> When I look at your heavens,
>   the work of your fingers,
>   the moon and the stars that you have established;
> what are human beings that you are mindful of them,
>   mortals that you care for them?

The psalmist could not have the remotest notion of the real immensity of the heavens. But he could stand, as we do, under the moonlit, starlit sky and see for himself what diminutive things humans are. Why should God be bothered with us? Must we not be beneath the Creator's notice?

If we are surprised to find here something of our own disquiet in the mysterious universe, we may be even more surprised to find, too, a little of our own aggressiveness toward nature. What is a human being? The psalmist answers his own question: Humans are little less than gods, crowned with glory and honor, since God has given them dominion over the earth and put all things under human feet—"sheep and oxen,/. . . the beasts of the field,/the birds of the air, and the fish of the sea." May we see in the present-day conquest of space an extension of humanity's divine commission to subdue the earth and to have dominion because we are made in the image and likeness of God?

When you come to think about it, the psalmists were very "modern": caught, as we are, between admiration for humanity and a sense of human littleness, between self-congratulation and self-doubt—either way, wondrously fascinated, as humans always have been, with themselves.

But if the diagnosis is apt—if this is what it is to be human, lost in space but never quite believing it—what shall we do about it?

III

In their *Lessons of History*, a volume that sums up two lifetimes of historical study, Will and Ariel Durant make a telling point: "Generations of men establish a growing mastery over the earth, but they are destined to become fossils in its soil." For some of you, that thought, if you dwell on it too long, may take a bit of the excitement out of humanity's struggle with physical nature—if, in the end, it is a struggle we must lose. Is our only advantage that, at least with the tops of our heads, we *know* we must lose, whereas the universe knows nothing of its victory? For myself, I find that rather chilly comfort. Is there then no other?

Perhaps there are a few strenuous spirits for whom the sheer sense of adventure is the only antidote needed for the feeling of human insignificance. Or perhaps we should exercise our unique human freedom to create worlds of our own imagination, more pleasant to live in than the unfeeling world of astronomy and physics. Or perhaps the only sensible course is to shake a fist at nature before we go under.

But what does our psalmist say? One cannot help noticing that, just at the moment when he has felt his "estrangement," it is, for him, the question of God's Word that arises. "I am a stranger on the earth: hide not Thy commandments from me." He cries out for a *word* from the silence. Now, if the word *you* would like to hear is that we really are, after all, divine—our sense of nothingness just a bad, passing dream—you had better not turn to your Psalter for reassurance. Though that other psalmist could exclaim, in a moment of pardonable exuberance, that we are made "little less than God," still the limit is not crossed, here or anywhere in basic biblical religion: from everlasting to everlasting *God* is God, and turns mortals back into the dust (Ps. 90:2–3).

No, our psalmist finds the basis of his confidence somewhere else: in the remarkable thought that breaks through in Ps. 119:114: "You are my hiding place and my shield;/I hope in your word" (cf. Ps. 32:7). If he calls God his "hiding place," may we not infer that the word from the silence is simply this: home is not the world as such, but God? And is this not the same word that we find in others of the psalms: that *God* is our dwelling place and our habitation (Ps. 90:1; 92:9; cf. Deut. 33:27, RSV)? It is the psalmist's sense of not quite belonging in the world that makes him perceive he belongs to Another. If he does not feel at home in the world, that is because the earth is only the "house of [his] pilgrimage" (v. 54, KJV), not his home. And don't be put off by the image of the pilgrimage just because pilgrims have sometimes got their geography wrong: the psalmist knew exactly where home was.

I can still vividly recall the powerful impression made on my then youthful mind when I first read the eloquent essay of Bertrand Russell (1872–1970), "A Free Man's Worship," and its stern admonition that "we must learn, each one of us, that the world was not made for us." If I did not find the admonition wholly devastating, that was because I had learned the same lesson already from a very old catechism. I will not tell you who wrote it (that might not strengthen my case), but it begins like this:

> What is the chief end of human life?
> > It is to know God.
> Why do you say that?
> > Because he has created us and put us in the world to be glorified in us. And there is good reason why we should devote our life to his glory: because he is the beginning of it.
> And what is the highest *good* of man?
> > The same thing . . . because without it our condition is more miserable than that of the brute-beasts.

I can certainly charge you to go out, with all the learning you have acquired, and to subdue the earth: it is your divine commission (Gen. 1:26). But remember, fellow strangers, that the world you subdue is not your home; it is only the house of your pilgrimage. And take time to make your peace with the mysterious creativeness that produced both your world and you. If the psalmist is right, it is not so unfriendly as the "passionate skeptic" believed: it sends the rain and makes the sun to rise even upon the skeptic. And may God hide neither the divine word nor the divine commandment from you!

The Simple Truth

"Spoiled . . . so he made it again."
Jeremiah 18:4

I had just missed my bus. Knowing there would be a long wait, I wandered over to see why the crowd was gathering. The reason turned out to be a street-corner evangelist. I was immediately spotted by an alert member of the team, who moved smartly around the outside of the circle and had me by the sleeve before I could escape. He gave me a quick, well-rehearsed sermon, and demanded to know if I was saved.

I assured him I was, and he smiled happily. Then I added that I was in fact a minister. The smile vanished, and he began to outline the plan of salvation all over again.

When I finally extricated myself, mumbling some excuse about having to catch a bus, I went my way wondering why I felt slightly irritated. It wasn't that I minded being identified as a poor, lost clergyman—though I'm glad I didn't mention I am also a theologian.

It wasn't that I was in any way put off by the question whether I was saved. I don't think that's a bad question. Some times are better than others for asking it, but anyone who stops to listen to an evangelist can hardly judge the question out of place.

What irritated me, at least to begin with, was a certain glibness about the rather mechanical sermonette. Being saved sounded altogether routine and uncomplicated, and it was offered to as though my assent to it would spare me any further worries as long as I lived. And I am programmed by temperament and training to doubt whether that could be so.

I

But, on reflection, I couldn't help asking myself, Are the popular evangelists entirely mistaken when they commend to us the *simple* gospel? As academics, we make it a duty to be skeptical, to distrust simplicity, to create difficulties everywhere. And quite rightly. To think critically is one of the prime benefits of education, or should be. Very well. But the mistake we often fall into is to imagine that the purpose of our thinking is not to understand the simplicity of faith, but to find some clever substitute for it. The gospel really does call for childlike trust. Otherwise, the church would be divided into lower-level *believers* and upper-level *thinkers;* and the grace of God, who wants to save us by faith, would be frustrated. The way things really are, Jesus could pray: "I thank you, Father, Lord of heaven and earth, because you have hidden these things from the wise and the intelligent and revealed them to infants; yes, Father, for such was your gracious will" (Matt. 11:25–26).

The really wise and intelligent among us want to understand what has been revealed to infants, themselves included. Even those who have become adult in thinking remain, in a sense, children in believing, since what life demands of all of us is a certain faith or trust. And even the profoundest and most subtle of theologies remain at their core, if they are Christian, accounts of the simplicity of faith.

It must therefore be possible for us to state, in all simplicity, what it is that we believe. Even if we would not do it in just the same words as the popular evangelist with his plan of salvation, I would like to think that my faith, in the end, is no different from his.

II

Now, one reason that the wise and the intelligent often miss the simplicity of faith and look past it for something else is because faith is given, first of all, not in ideas and arguments but in stories, in images, and even in common events that only seers, poets, and prophets grasp as revelation.

Take Jeremiah's striking image of the potter and the clay, suggested by a commonplace happening to which most of us would have given no more than a casual glance. Looking back, he testified that he had been sent: it was the prompting of God that took him down to the potter's house, to receive God's Word. The prophet obeyed. But in the potter's house he found nothing more than he had witnessed a dozen times before.

Methods of making pottery don't change much over the years; the essentials remain much the same today as they were in Jeremiah's day. Clay dug from the earth's surface had to be made smooth and pliable by kneading it with the hands, treading it underfoot, or beating it with wooden mallets. Stray stones or anything else that might hinder the potter's busy fingers had to be carefully removed. Then the clay was turned into a soft paste by adding water. It was ready for the potter's hands. Jeremiah's potter most likely worked with two stone wheels or discs joined together: the heavy, lower one he spun with his feet, and on the upper one he turned the soft clay.

Jeremiah noticed that the desired vessel was not made all at once. Something went wrong; perhaps the clay was still too stiff, or perhaps a stone had accidentally been left in it. The vessel was spoiled. But the potter immediately squeezed the clay into a shapeless lump and began again. That was all Jeremiah saw, and he had seen it often enough before.

But this time the word of the Lord came to him. A commonplace event became a revelation: "Then the word of the LORD came to me: Can I not do with you, O house of Israel, just as this potter has done? . . . Just like the clay in the potter's hand, so are you in my hand" (vv. 5–6).

"Spoiled . . . so he made it again" (v. 4); or, as the Revised Standard Version says, "He reworked it into another vessel." Jeremiah's prophecy was addressed to the people of Israel, but his words express the simple truth for believers everywhere. The meaning lies on the surface: it requires no great subtlety to draw it out. The story

is about the making, the spoiling, and the remaking of a
vessel.

III

Notice, first of all, the *making* of the vessel. It is being
turned out by the care and skill of a master craftsman.
True, the image of the potter and the clay has often been
used to admonish the unruly of the absolute power of God
rather than of God's loving care. The clay, it is pointed
out, is passive in the potter's hand, who can make of it
whatever he or she pleases: a twist of the wrist, a turn of
the hand, and the clay assumes a new shape. The potter
can make, unmake, and remake the vessel—or can even
throw it away.

This is in fact how another prophet, Isaiah, used the
image of the potter and the clay. Shall the thing made talk
back to its maker (Isa. 29:16; 45:9)? The Apostle Paul,
quoting Isaiah, heightens the severity of the image, asking: What if God, to show God's power, made some vessels for destruction? Can the vessels lodge a complaint
against their creator? (See Rom. 9:22–23.)

Paul's use of the potter and the clay has been described
as "one of the most heart-sickening shifts of a false theology." Well, perhaps it would be if the similitude stood for
nothing else but the irresistible, sovereign might of God.
But it means a great deal more than that. Recall another
description of the potter at work, this time in Sirach:

> The potter sitting at his work
> and turning the wheel with his feet;
> . . . is always deeply concerned over his products.
> . . . .
> He sets his heart to finish the glazing."
> (38:29–30)

That the potter has power over the clay is a salutary truth,
but it is not the whole truth; the potter is also the embod-
iment of skill, loving attention, and singleness of purpose.

Fundamental to the simplicity of faith is, first of all, the
deep persuasion that through all the events that crowd in

on us—pleasant and painful, good and bad—our lives are being shaped, molded, fashioned. We are, of course, ready to admit that finally we do not make our world or our destiny, but receive them. And yet we are not passive objects either. There would be no point in telling us we are clay in the potter's hand if we were in the grip of an inexorable fate. A prophecy is not a taunt or a curse. The man and the woman of faith apprehend their daily existence not simply as their fate but as opportunity, support, care. This is what they hear in the words: "Can I not do with you . . . as this potter has done?" (v. 6) Vessels, *persons*, are being made. That's the first point.

But notice, second, the *spoiling* of the vessel. The parable offers us no deep theological explanation of what goes wrong, or why, only the simple observation that the vessel is spoiled. The fault is evidently assigned to the material, not to the craftsman. Beyond that, there is only the fact, and not a theory: "The vessel he was making of clay was spoiled in the potter's hand" (v. 4).

Jeremiah is speaking of the apostasy of God's chosen people. Their fault is stated in v. 12: "We will follow our own plans, and each of us will act according to the stubbornness of our evil will." Once again we can see that the point of the prophecy is not to predict the inevitable; it is a call to conversion, so that disaster may be averted. The image of the potter and the clay holds out the possibility of repentance, and the possibility of repentance bespeaks the potter's care. This is what Jeremiah's prophecy says explicitly, at least as the text has come down to us: "I am . . . devising a plan against you"; therefore, "Amend your ways and your doings" (v. 11).

And that is the second thing in the simplicity of faith: the recognition that there is something in us, whatever it is, that frustrates the molding of our lives for good, and the goal is missed. The clay resists the potter's hands, so that the potter does not realize the intended design in it all at once. The man and woman of faith grasp their daily experience as a daily call to conversion. Vessels, persons, are being made—and spoiled.

Notice, third, the *remaking* of the vessel: "Spoiled . . .

so he made it again" (v. 4). Jeremiah has been nicknamed "the gloomy prophet," and the word "jeremiad" has passed into our vocabulary as a tale of unmitigated woe. In the very next chapter, he has another story about a spoiled vessel. He bought an earthen flask from the potter, took it to the valley of the son of Hinnom, broke it in pieces on the rubbish dump, and announced to the bystanders: "Thus says the LORD of hosts: So will I break this people and this city, as one breaks a potter's vessel, so that it can never be mended" (19:11).

A message of gloom and doom? A jeremiad? Not entirely, for a message wholly without hope would be a message wholly without point. The point in chapter 19 remains what it is in chapter 18: Vessels can be remade—however, it is infinitely more difficult when they have been through the firing kiln and have become hard and brittle.

If the vessel is spoiled while still in the hand of the potter, it is not thrown aside. The potter squeezes the clay, begins again, and works patiently until satisfied.

The third affirmation of a simple faith, then, is that when things go wrong, as they will, the past is not irrevocable. New events, new resources can always overcome the fateful power of old events. And while it is true, as Jeremiah elsewhere puts it, that the Ethiopian cannot change his own skin, or the leopard his own spots (13:23), it is also true that the clay never falls from the potter's hands, who can do with it what it cannot do for itself. Vessels, persons, are being made, spoiled—and made again.

IV

"Spoiled . . . so he made it again." For us, these words are not only an Old Testament allegory, but also an apt description of the New Testament gospel. The work of the Savior, of which we read in the Gospels, was precisely the remaking of spoiled vessels, the mending of broken, unfulfilled lives. And it has been just the same throughout the entire history of the church, whenever the word of Christ has been heard again—in the pages of the New

Testament, in the ministrations of the church, or in the conversation of friends—saying, "Take heart, son; your sins are forgiven," or, "Take heart, daughter; your faith has made you well" (Matt. 9:2, 22).

The new vessel, the new creation, is *Christ's* work; the power of the new life comes to us from him (2 Cor. 5:17). That's a plain fact, repeated thousands of times over the centuries of church history; and it is a fact worth infinitely more than the half-dozen theories that have tried to explain it. It's the simple truth. And it will give the wise and the intelligent more than enough to think about for a very long time.

One Thing Certain

"One thing I do know,
that though I was blind, now I see."
John 9:25

Sydney Harris has said that "the basic aim of higher education is only twofold: to train one to put, and prepare one to answer, two questions: 'What do you mean?' and 'How do you know?'" That's not a bad statement of what we are about in this place of higher learning. And it would be scandalous if, educated as we are, we tried to shield our religion from these two searching questions.

True, we are told in the Scriptures that unless we become as little children, we will never enter the kingdom of heaven (Matt. 18:3). But we are also told not to remain like children, but to grow up (Eph. 4:14–15)—to "be infants in evil, but in thinking be adults" (1 Cor. 14:20).

The path to a mature faith is sometimes painful. It is as much a process of unlearning as of learning. In this sense we might agree with the words of the *Tao-te-ching*:

> The student learns by daily increment,
> The Way is gained by daily loss,
> Loss upon loss until
> At last comes rest.

When I was just beginning the theological part of my education, the minister of my church admitted to me and a friend that he nursed just enough doubt to keep him on his toes. We were shocked, and we went back to our college shaking our heads and wringing our hands in disapproval. We had no doubts. We thought we knew.

But there is nothing like a theological education to show you that you don't really know as much as you thought you knew. Indeed, any education teaches us to carry our convictions back to secure premises—"until at last comes rest." But if that is so, where do you start rebuilding the house of faith, when the foundations have begun to shake?

I

Perhaps there isn't just one starting point. We have to find the way for ourselves and "always be ready to make [a] defense to anyone who demands from [us] an accounting for the hope that is in [us]; yet do it with gentleness and reverence" (1 Peter 3:15–16).

There are devout Christians who don't even see the problem, because they have bolted the door and secured the windows against an unbelieving world outside, changing nothing within, not so much as rearranging the old furniture. I think this is unwise; it courts disaster. . . . But I have no doubt that their faith in God may very well be genuine.

There are those who would find their faith strengthened by some tangible token of the divine: if, say, the Shroud of Turin turned out to be authentic—the actual garment in which the crucified Lord was laid to rest. I think that too is a mistake, for the reason that Erasmus (c.1469–1536) gave four centuries ago when speaking of another sacred relic: "If anyone displays the tunic of Christ, to what corner of the earth shall we not hasten so that we may kiss it? Yet were you to bring forth his entire wardrobe, it would not manifest Christ more clearly and truly than the Gospel writings." Well said! But I don't doubt that a proper reverence for Christ can be deepened and exercised in what seem to me improper ways.

There are those who believe that faith will rest easier if they can only prove the existence of God, or establish the plain facts about the historical Jesus—both difficult tasks, and you will make quite a name for yourself if you succeed in either one. I admire the zeal of these seekers after proof, and I wish them well. But I think the skeptic Anthony Collins (1676–1729) had a point when he said of one of them: "Nobody doubted the existence of God until Dr. Clarke strove to prove it."

Others again are ready to trust their faith to some approved authority, whether a book or a church. But that, of course, is just where the problem of our coming of age lies. "If I have a book which understands for me, a pastor who has a conscience for me . . . I need not think, provided I can pay." The words are from Immanuel Kant (1724–1804). But what he says of thinking, Martin Luther (1483–1546) had already said of believing: All must do their own believing, as surely as all must do their own dying. And yet, I would not wish to deny that the one who turns to an authority may very well, even by this route, do his or her own believing in God.

Most winsome of all is the calm assurance of devout believers like the English physicist and Quaker Sir Arthur Eddington (1882–1944). His daily commerce with God fully satisfied his need for the assurance that, in reaching out to the unseen world, he was not following an illusion. "The most flawless proof for the existence of God," he says, "is no substitute for [this actual relationship with God]; and if we have [it], the most convincing disproof is turned harmlessly aside. If I may say it with reverence, the soul and God laugh together over so odd a conclusion." But not all of us can claim such familiarity with the Supreme Being that we could share a joke; that there are some who can only multiplies the sorrow of those who can't.

I repeat, I have no wish to deny that any or all of these moves may open the lines of communication between the soul and God; and for this we can be thankful. But the risk, at least, is that Christian faith may not be strengthened by them, but thrown off its true center. And where is that? Is there somewhere else where our thoughts can finally come to rest?

II

The answer lies in that remarkable passage from the Gospel of John that we read as our Scripture lesson—in

two parts because it is very long, but too good not to read
it whole (John 9:1–23, 24–41). The story has a lively, dramatic, and even ironic quality unexcelled in any other
passage of Scripture. As usual, John makes of the stories
current in the Christian community an allegory of spiritual truth, replete with detailed symbolism. He signals his
intent with the words of Jesus in verse 5: "I am the light
of the world."

No doubt, John has partly in mind the passing of the
light from the old religion to the new: the man born blind
is driven out (v. 34), excommunicated, and Jesus finds him
and takes him into the new fellowship. The symbol of water and the man's eventual profession of faith are perhaps
echoes of early Christian baptism.

But we do not go wrong if we say that the man represents us all, blind in sin from the day he was born (cf. v. 2).
The Pharisees (or "the Jews") are religious authorities
everywhere, so sure of their better-than-20/20 vision that
they cannot discern a new fact right under their noses.
The parents too, though in this drama they act out of fear,
play a universal role, since they recognize that they can no
longer speak for their son. "He is of age; ask him" (v. 23).

Look more closely at the Pharisees. From the first, they
are more interested in *how* the man has received his sight
than in the fact that he has received it (v. 15). Actually, the
means used—clay made of earth and spittle—was less
strange in their world than it would be in ours. But I am reminded of Dwight L. Moody's appearance before some English churchmen during one of his evangelistic campaigns in
Britain. What they didn't care for, they said, was his way of
doing things. To which he replied that he didn't much care
for it either, but preferred it to their way of *not* doing things.

We read next of the Pharisees that there is a division
among them (v. 16). And that certainly has the ring of
truth about it: where two or three theologians are gathered together, there you have a division. But the Pharisees
all agree in worrying because the cure has been effected
on the Sabbath. John Calvin (1509–64) comments: "The
words of the Law enjoin men to abstain from their own
works [on the Sabbath], not from the works of God." A

good point! Or may the light of the world shine only six days a week?

And now—most important—notice the contrast between the Pharisees and the man born blind. The Pharisees appeal to the authority of their Scriptures (that is, to Moses) and to ecclesiastical authority (their own: "You were born entirely in sins, and are you trying to teach us?" v. 34). The man, by contrast, has a single fact, and he sticks to it tenaciously: He can see! "One thing I do know, that though I was blind, now I see" (v. 25). That, to him, was the one thing certain. And it is not so very different for ourselves.

III

We too have come to see our world in the light Jesus casts on it. That is why we find ourselves in this great chapel in the midst of a proud university—miles and years removed from the carpenter's son in Nazareth. Our vision may not have been given to us so dramatically as the blind man's; it may have come to us gradually, even imperceptibly, over the years. But for us, too, it is a matter of actual fact that we see by the light that comes to us down the centuries from Nazareth.

Of course we appeal to the Bible and the church. But we do so because in the Scriptures and in the church the crucified Lord, who lives again in the company of the faithful, has met us. He has, as a matter of fact, determined the way we see our world, quickening our perception of life's goodness and life's demands.

When we have fallen, it is the image of the great physician that, as a matter of fact, has raised us up again with the words "Take heart . . . ; your sins are forgiven" (Matt. 9:2) and "Those who are well have no need of a physician" (v. 12).

When we have grown lax and indifferent to our moral debts, it is the image of the son of man in his glory that, as a matter of fact, has stabbed us awake with the terrible words: "I was hungry and you gave me no food, I was thirsty and you gave me nothing to drink" (Matt. 25:42).

Here, in this certain Lordship of Christ over our lives, is the actual bond between Christians: by it we recognize one another across the dividing lines that separate creed from creed and one denomination from another. The preacher has no higher task than to bring to consciousness and to nurture what every Christian in his or her heart thus knows; and the theologian has no higher task than to attempt to understand it.

Jesus has become for us *in fact* the light of our world, and none of the other things we have spoken of are as certain as his Lordship over our lives, however fragmentary, partial, and imperfect it may still be. His claim on us needs no other authorization; rather, those other authorities borrow whatever light they may have from him.

IV

And who is this who has become for us the light of the world? If you can confess, with the ancient church, that he is very God and very man, two natures in one person, the second Person of the blessed Trinity, well and good. But if not, then begin where the blind man began, not where the ancient church ended.

First, he speaks only of "the man called Jesus" (John 9:11). He knows nothing about him, not even where to find him. "They said to him, 'Where is he?' He said, 'I do not know'" (v. 12).

Next, he decides that the one who has opened his eyes must be a prophet (v. 17), perhaps because Jesus, like the prophets, showed a remarkable freedom over against the established religion. But the man doesn't know whether or not Jesus is a sinner—only that now he can see (v. 25). And he begins to think of himself as one of Jesus' disciples: "Do you *also*," he asks the Pharisees, "want to become his disciples?" (v. 27).

The third conclusion is that Jesus must come from God, or he could not do what he has done (v. 33).

And, finally, when Jesus the Son of man seeks him out, he makes the Christian confession, "Lord, I believe," and worships him (v. 38). He has progressed from the gift of sight to an act of homage before the light of the world.

Whether the man paid Jesus divine honors is another question. I turned to Calvin's commentary for guidance, expecting that he, at least, would miss no opportunity to affirm the deity of Christ. But I was mistaken. The word "worshiped," Calvin says, means uncommon respect and homage, not that the man had recognized Christ as God manifest in the flesh.

What do you know? What do you really know? As far as our Christian faith is concerned, the one thing certain—as certain, really, as death and taxes—is that we see the world by the light that has come to us from Jesus. And, if we are not in too much of a hurry to reach the faith of Athanasius (c. 293–373), we will rejoice that there are many others, even outside our own folds, who heed the Good Shepherd's voice along with us (John 10:16)—all the way up to that uncommon respect and homage in the final act of the man born blind.

We don't claim to see everything. To the one thing certain must be added the "one thing . . . needful" (RSV) of which another of the Gospels tells us; and that is to sit at Jesus' feet and want to learn more (Luke 10:42). Even then, we are promised only enough light to walk and live by: "Again Jesus spoke to them, saying, 'I am the light of the world. Whoever follows me will never walk in darkness but will have the light of life'" (John 8:12).

Dreamers of the Day

(Convocation Sunday)

"Whatever is true, whatever is honorable, whatever is just, whatever is pure, whatever is pleasing, whatever is commendable, if there is any excellence and if there is anything worthy of praise, think about these things. Keep on doing the things that you have learned and received and heard and seen in me, and the God of peace will be with you."

Philippians 4:8–9

We had been talking about the latest movies. I have long since forgotten which, and I don't believe I myself had seen any of them. But I do remember that someone described a film with a happy ending, and that next someone else went on to review a very different film: crammed with violence, infidelity, and anguish, it ended in unrelieved gloom. And I remember, above all, the comment of one of my friends: "At least this one," he said, "was about real life." Like everyone else present, I nodded my assent; but almost immediately I had second thoughts.

Real life? What did it mean? Did that mean that more than 50 percent of our lives is R-rated or X-rated material? This wasn't true of ourselves, seated comfortably around a well-laden dinner table. We were all nice people, gainfully employed; most of us enjoyed good health; half of us were even still living with our first wife, or first husband, and, as far as I know, were not unhappy about it. What made us so ready to view the seamy, steamy parts of human existence as "real life"?

Perhaps my friend was simply expressing his own personal sense of injustice. He had a right to it. He had

struggled out of a broken marriage, and his medical history made him fearful that he was living on borrowed
time. Real life doesn't deal out good things and bad
things evenhandedly; and a man can't be expected to balance against his own harsh lot, if such it is, all the good
things bestowed on someone else. But why, then, were
the rest of us so quick to give our assent, if to us life had
been so much kinder?

I

Well, perhaps we all instinctively agree with Blaise
Pascal (1623–62) that, however happy the rest of the play
has been, the last act is always tragic: "A little earth is
thrown upon our head, and that is the end forever." The
wife of Bertrand Russell's (1872–1970) biographer, Alan
Wood, remarked how unjust it would be if all the young
men killed in war were to have no second chance to attain
happiness. Russell answered: "But the universe *is* unjust. . . .
[T]he secret of happiness is to face the fact that the world is
horrible, horrible, *horrible*. . . . You must feel it deeply and
not brush it aside . . . and then you can start being happy
again."

You may think that the universe was in fact unusually
kind to Russell; but admittedly it wasn't, and isn't, to the
victims of natural and human-made calamities. Whatever
you think about life, you have to take its negative side into
your reckoning. And then, of course, there's also a tedium
to real life that you can't overlook either.

II

I was still meditating on real life as I made my way
home after the dinner party. My thoughts called up a
long-forgotten occasion much farther back in my mind,
from my student days in England. The size of my scholarship allowance had been immutably fixed sometime in
the fifteenth century, and to stretch it out I had gone to
work with a painting and decorating contractor. It was a
cold, damp November day in mid-August, and I was up a

ladder sanding a windowsill. (I wasn't trusted with a paint-brush.) Down below, the owner of the house remarked to my father, who had stopped by, what a fine thing it was for a student to plant his feet occasionally in the "real world."

So this was reality! I had found it at last: a ladder, a scrap of sandpaper, and six pounds ten a week. What was I doing at Cambridge, then? The real world, so the prag-matist argues, is where you earn a living; and you get a col-lege degree to ensure it will be as comfortable a living as possible. These days, you can't be too sure. Sometimes, as the book of Proverbs says, "Hope deferred makes the heart sick" (Prov. 13:12).

But back then, I denied the pragmatist the premise of his argument. I wasn't worried about a job when the paper chase was over; with the blessing of a classical education, I believed that the only real world, undiminished by perpet-ual decay, was the world of ideas and ideals. Naive, youthful daydreaming perhaps. But I still don't think I was entirely wrong. There's more than one kind of daydreaming.

III

If I may take you back to the movies again: Recall, for a moment, the enchanting film *Chariots of Fire*, which won the Oscar for best picture in 1981. That one I did see, and I went back again to find out why it captivated me the first time. It claims to be the true story of two men utterly committed to the same goal, but for very different rea-sons.

Both have set their hearts on an Olympic gold medal. But for Harold Abrahams, running—or rather winning— is a weapon against anti-Semitism; and for Eric Liddell, running is a doxology, because when he runs he feels God's pleasure. Abrahams, fiercely competitive ("If I can't win, I won't run"), trains grimly and intensely, with rigid professional discipline; Liddell, quietly self-possessed, breaks every rule and runs as naturally as a wild animal. For each of them running is an extension of individual character. But for both, Abrahams gets it exactly right when he affirms his belief in the "relentless pursuit of excellence."

The message of *Chariots of Fire* was taken up enthusiastically by a surprising variety of critics. They said that it "lifts the spirits"; that it is "an uncompromising vision of the human spirit," "an inspiring story of aspiration and accomplishment," and so on. One remarked that "it's about time we had a chance to see so positive a film."

Some went overboard, I suppose. Said one: "It's the affirmation of all that's great in the human spirit." As I understood it, there was more to the picture than that: There were clear, if gentle, hints that venerable universities and the Olympic Games aren't the whole world, that they are havens of privilege and elitism, and that even on the inside all is not well: prejudice, complacency, and ambiguous motives hide behind all the civility. There are different gods and different mountaintops, and in 1924 old ideals are beginning to crumble. "Perhaps, sir," says Abrahams to the master of Trinity College, "you would rather I played the gentleman—and lost?"

Not the whole world. No, but the point, I take it, is that here was a corner of the world where you would have found ideals and heroes, values and commitment, in short, the pursuit of excellence. One forbidden word near the beginning of the film raised the rating to PG; thereafter, it was surprisingly clean. And the undercurrent of criticism never became cynical. If anything, the mood was nostalgic. And if it seemed old-fashioned, that may have been in part a comment on the audience.

IV

"If there is any excellence and if there is anything worthy of praise, think about these things." Enclosed as they are between some very practical concerns, Paul's words are a call to reflect on ideals in the midst of actual existence. And if we listen also to the prophets, we are even summoned to dream a little.

Isaiah dreamed of a time of *health and wholeness*, when the eyes of the blind will be opened and the ears of the deaf unstopped; when the lame man will leap like a hart, and the dumb will sing for joy (Isa. 35:5–6).

Jeremiah saw a day of *justice*, when the law of the Lord will no longer be written on tablets of stone, but in the hearts of the people (Jer. 31:31).

Ezekiel was shown the coming *rebirth* of the nation, when the dry bones in the valley will hear the word of the Lord and live (Ezek. 37:1–14).

Micah's vision was a vision of *peace*, of swords beaten into plowshares and spears into pruning hooks (Micah 4:3).

Habakkuk's was a vision of *truth:* "The earth will be filled/with the knowledge of the glory of the LORD,/as the waters cover the sea" (Hab. 2:14).

And Joel foresaw the *pouring out of God's spirit* on all flesh, so that your sons and daughters will prophesy, your old men will dream dreams, and your young men will see visions (Joel 2:28; cf. Acts 2:17).

In this way, the abstractions that Paul bids us keep in mind—truth, justice, and all the rest—engage our hearts and fire our imaginations. Joan of Arc testifies in Bernard Shaw's play: "I hear voices telling me what to do. They come from God." Robert de Baudricourt: "They come from your imagination." Joan: "Of course. That is how the messages of God come to us."

Dreams, of course. But these are the dreams that real life in the real world is made of; and they can raise us to a relative independence from what is, after all, not the real world but only the actual world given to us as the material of our calling. Without such dreams a student, a scholar, a scientist, a doctor, a lawyer, a politician, a poet, or anyone else may very well find that what he or she does has become not a calling but a "living" (falsely so called), which lacks the energy to survive tedium and adversity and the cynicism they can bring. In short, as the proverb says in that inspired mistranslation of the King James Version: "Where there is no vision, the people perish" (Prov. 29:18).

Christians have no monopoly on such dreams and visions. Even Paul's exhortation to the Philippians sounds amazingly like the commonplace thoughts of the pagan moralists, right down to his choice of words for excellence (v. 8) and self-sufficiency (v. 11). But there *is* a difference. To be religious is precisely to be convinced that we are never more firmly in touch with reality than when we, like Paul, are "not disobedient to the heavenly vision" (Acts 26:19). And to be Christian is to see our obedience as homage to the Savior, at whose name, in Paul's own vision, every knee should bow (Phil. 2:10).

T. E. Lawrence wrote: "All men dream. . . . They who dream by night in the dusty recesses of their minds wake in the day to find that it is vanity; but the dreamers of the day are dangerous men, for they act their dream with open eyes, to make it possible." Well, not dangerous, I hope, but men and women to be reckoned with.

NOTES AND FURTHER READING

As observed in the Editor's Introduction, B. A. Gerrish has written extensively on the major themes of Christian theology and the impact of modern thought on its expression. For those readers who desire further elucidation of these themes, references to his other writings are given here, in reverse order of publication, below the sources of his citations. It should be noted that, with the possible exception of *A Prince of the Church*, the works listed are of a scholarly nature. While Gerrish's lucid prose makes them accessible to a wide audience, the treatment is markedly different from that of the present volume. Gerrish's forthcoming work on Christian dogmatics will be of particular interest to readers as it provides a developed and systematic treatment of all the themes contained in this volume.

Editor's Introduction

For further discussion of the concept of the sacramental Word, see: Mary T. Stimming, " 'New Nazareths in Us': Towards a Sacramental Word Interpretation of Lutheran, Reformed, and Roman Catholic Doctrines of the Means of Grace" (Ph.D. diss., University of Chicago, 1996) and Dawn DeVries, *Jesus Christ in the Preaching of Calvin and Schleiermacher*, Columbia Series in Reformed Theology (Louisville, Ky.: Westminster John Knox Press, 1996).

I. THE JOURNEY

The Face of God (15 March 1992)

John Calvin, *Commentary on Isaiah* 42:14, 49:15; *Institutes of the Christian Religion* 3.2.13, 2.28 (cited in the 1559 edition by book, chapter, and section). Seneca, *De providentia*, I.i.5–6. Martin Luther, *Commentary on Genesis* ad loc. Nina Herrmann Donnelley, *Go Out in Joy!* (Atlanta: John Knox Press, 1977), pp. 107, 161, 215. See further Gerrish, *Grace and Gratitude: The Eucharistic Theology of John Calvin* (Minneapolis: Fortress Press, 1993); "The Mirror of God's Goodness: A Key Metaphor in Calvin's View of Man," in *The Old Protestantism and the New: Essays on the*

Reformation Heritage (Chicago: University of Chicago Press; Edinburgh: T. & T. Clark, 1982), pp. 150–59; "Theology within the Limits of Piety Alone: Schleiermacher and Calvin's Notion of God," in *The Old Protestantism and the New*, pp. 196–207.

Forgiveness (17 May 1992)

The hymn mentioned is "Great God of Wonders," by Samual Davies. The Martin Buber comment about Jesus in relation to the Pharisees can be found in his book *Two Types of Faith*, trans. Norman P. Goldhawk (New York: Collier Books, 1986). The Augustine quotation is in *A Select Library of the Nicene and Post-Nicene Fathers of the Christian Church*, ed. Philip Schaff, 14 vols. (Grand Rapids: Wm. B. Eerdmans Publishing Co., 1969–75), 6:417. The story of the saint's vision is mentioned by H. R. Mackintosh, *The Christian Experience of Forgiveness* (New York: Harper & Brothers, 1927). See further Gerrish, *Grace and Gratitude*.

Gratitude (6 March 1994)

Augustine's remarks on faith in relation to the text are in his treatise *On the Predestination of the Saints*, III.7–10, *A Select Library of the Nicene and Post-Nicene Fathers of the Christian Church*, ed. Philip Schaff, 14 vols. (Grand Rapids: Wm. B. Eerdmans Publishing Co., 1969–75), 5:500–503. The quotation from Milton is from the second part of *Paradise Lost*. *What Americans Believe* was published by the Bana Research Group (Glendale, Calif., 1991). Lucretius, *On the Nature of Things*, book 3, line 971. See further Gerrish, *Grace and Gratitude*; "The Mirror of God's Goodness."

II. HINDRANCES

Truth from the Road (3 February 1985)

The sad exchange concerning the baby born with brain damage appeared in the Ann Landers column, *Chicago Sun-Times*, 11 May 1984. John A. Mackay, *A Preface to Christian Theology* (London: Nisbet & Co., 1942), esp. pp. 29, 44, 39. See further Gerrish, "Practical Belief: Friedrich Karl Forberg and the Fictionalist View of Religious Language," in *Continuing the Reformation: Essays on Modern Religious Thought* (Chicago: University of Chicago Press, 1993), pp. 127–43.

Evil at the Hand of God? (10 April 1983)

Harold Kushner, *When Bad Things Happen to Good People*, rev. ed. (New York: Schocken Books, 1989), pp. 127, 129. See further Gerrish, *A Prince of the Church: Schleiermacher and the Beginnings of Modern Theology* (Philadelphia: Fortress Press; London: SCM Press, 1984).

The View from Eternity (8 May 1988)

John Calvin, *Institutes of the Christian Religion* 3.2.17. The account of Kant's death is from Will Durant, *The Story of Philosophy: The Lives and Opinions of Greater Philosophers* (New York: Pocket Books, 1954), p. 286. G. W. Leibniz quotation from *Theodicy: Essays on the Goodness of God, the Freedom of Man, and the Origin of Evil*, ed. Austin Farrer, trans. E. M. Huggard (London: Routledge & Kegan Paul, [1952]), p. 130. See further Gerrish, *A Prince of the Church*; "The Secret Religion of Germany: Christian Piety and the Pantheism Controversy," in *Continuing the Reformation*, pp. 109–26.

III. THE LIGHTBEARER
"Many Infallible Proofs" (31 March 1991)

Arthur T. Pierson, *"Many Infallible Proofs": The Evidences of Christianity* (New York: F. H. Revell, 1886), p. 11. Samuel Butler, *The Way of All Flesh* (London: J. Cape, [1926]), chap. 59. William Paley, *View of the Evidences of Christianity* (1794). See further Gerrish, "Jesus, Myth, and History: Troeltsch's Stand in the 'Christ-Myth' Debate," in *The Old Protestantism and the New*, pp. 230–47.

The Christ of Faith (1 May 1994)

Walter Schwarz, "Man and Myth—More Bad News for Believers," appeared in the *Guardian Weekly*, 18 October 1992. For the rival representations of Jesus in the recent literature, see B. A. Gerrish, *Saving and Secular Faith: An Invitation to Systematic Theology* (Minneapolis: Fortress Press, 1999), chap. 6. The quotations from Rudolf Bultmann and John Calvin are from their respective commentaries ad loc. See further Gerrish, "Jesus, Myth, and History."

The Living Word (27 November 1988)

The "eighteenth-century skeptic" mentioned is Friedrich Karl Forberg (1770–1848). Ernest Sutherland Bates, ed., *The Bible Designed to Be Read as Literature* (London: William Heinemann, [1936]). For the remarks by Ralph Waldo Emerson, see Robert O. Ballou, ed., *The Bible of the World* (New York: Viking, 1939), p. xvi. The Erasmus quotation is taken from his *Paraclesis* (the preface to his Greek and Latin edition of the New Testament, [1516]); this text can be found in English in John C. Olin, ed., *Christian Humanism and the Reformation: Selected Writings of Erasmus with the Life of Erasmus by Beatus Rhenanus*, rev. ed. (New York: Fordham University Press, 1975), p. 106. The comments from John Calvin can be found in the Preface to Olivétan's New Testament (1535/43), trans. in *Calvin's Commentaries*, ed. Joseph Haroutunian, Library of Christian Classics (Philadelphia: Westminster Press, 1958), vol. 23: 70. Emil Brunner, *Our Faith* (London: SCM Press, 1936), pp. 19–20. See further Gerrish, "The Word of God and the Words of Scripture: Luther and Calvin on Biblical Authority," in *The Old Protestantism and the New*, pp. 51–68; on Forberg, see "Practical Belief."

The Preeminence of Christ *(21 February 1993)*

Evelyn Underhill, *The Mystic Way: A Psychological Study in Christian Origins* (London: J. M. Dent & Sons, 1913), p. 118. Arthur Conan Doyle, *The New Revelation* (New York: George H. Doran Co., 1918), p. 61. Jerome's statement can be found in his commentary ad loc. See further Gerrish, "The Word of God and the Words of Scripture"; "Jesus, Myth, and History."

For and Against *(28 April 1985)*

Friedrich Schleiermacher, *Kleine Schriften und Predigten*, ed. Hayo Gerdes and Emanuel Hirsch, 3 vols. (Berlin: Walter de Gruyter, 1969–70), 3:31.

Christ the Kingmaker *(21 November 1993)*

Martin Luther, *On Christian Freedom*, in *Works of Martin Luther: Philadelphia Edition*, 6 vols. (Philadelphia: Muhlenberg Press, 1915–43), 2:323. John Calvin, *Institutes of the Christian Religion* 2.15.2, 3. Francis Bacon, *Essays*, Essay 1: "Of Truth." Sydney J. Harris, *The Best of Sydney Harris* (Boston: Houghton Mifflin Co., 1975), pp. 94–95. Epictetus, *Moral Discourses*, I.xvi.20. Viktor Frankl, *Man's Search for Meaning: An Introduction to Logotherapy*, trans. Ilse Lasch, 3d ed. (New York: Simon & Schuster, 1984), pp. 19, 136. W. E. Henley, "Invictus," in vol. 1 of *Poems, The Works of W. E. Henley*, 2 vols. (New York: AMS Press, 1970). The poem appears under "Echoes IV, 'Out of the night that covers me.'"

IV. TRANSFORMATION

Sin *(12 February 1979)*

Author's note: For the juxtaposition of my two texts—linked by the "How much more?" —my warrant lies in Hebrews 12:24, although Hebrews 9:14 actually makes its contrast with the blood of the sacrificial animals. J. B. Priestley, *An Inspector Calls* (London: Heinemann Educational Books, 1965). Karl Menninger, *Whatever Became of Sin?* (New York: Hawthorn Books, [1973]). Emil Brunner, *The Scandal of Christianity* (London: SCM Press, 1951), p. 65. Robert Burns, "Holy Willie's Prayer," in *The Poetical Works of Robert Burns*, 3 vol. in one (Boston: Houghton, Mifflin and Company, n.d.), p. 105.

Fitting God In (16 May 1993)

The statement attributed to Laplace is discussed in Roger Hahn's contribution to *God and Nature: Historical Essays on the Encounter between Christianity and Science*, ed. David C. Lindberg and Ronald L. Numbers (Berkeley: University of California Press, 1986); see p. 256. The Socratic aphorism is from the *Apology*. The remark of the visiting scientist is quoted from the Chicago *Tribune*, 12 November 1992. The hymn quoted is "Dear Lord and Father of Mankind," by John Greenleaf Whittier. See further Gerrish, "Nature and the Theater of Redemption: Schleiermacher on Christian Dogmatics and the Creation Story," in *Continuing the Reformation*, pp. 196–216; "'To the Unknown God': Luther and Calvin on the Hiddenness of God," in *The Old Protestantism and the New*, pp. 131–49; "The Reformation and the Rise of Modern Science," in *The Old Protestantism and the New*, pp. 163–78.

Grace Demanding (20 February 1983)

John Calvin, "Essay on the Lord's Supper," from *The Form of Prayers (1542 and 1545)*, in *Calvin's Ecclesiastical Advice*, trans. Mary Beaty and Benjamin W. Farley (Lousiville: Westminster/John Knox Press, 1991), pp. 165–70. Adolf von Harnack commented about the melancholy and easygoing types of Christian; see H. Martin Rumscheidt, *Revelation and Theology: An Analysis of the Barth-Harnack Correspondence of 1923* (Cambridge: Cambridge University Press, 1972), p. 19. The Heidelberg Catechism, in *Reformed Confessions of the 16th Century*, ed. Arthur C. Cochrane (Philadelphia: Westminster Press, 1966), pp. 305–31. The Isaac Watts hymn is "When I Survey the Wondrous Cross." See further Gerrish, *Saving and Secular Faith; Grace and Gratitude*.

V. RESPONSE

The Unquenchable Flame (6 March 1988; Bond Chapel)

Peter L. Berger, *A Rumor of Angels* (Garden City, N.Y.: Doubleday & Co., Anchor Books, 1970), p. 67. C. S. Lewis, *The*

Pilgrim's Regress, 3d ed. (London: Geoffrey Bles, 1945), pp. 21–22. John Calvin, *Geneva Catechism* in *Calvin: Theological Treatises*, trans. J. K. S. Reid, Library of Christian Classics, 26 vols. (Philadelphia: Westminster Press, 1954), 22:104. B. F. Westcott, commentary ad loc. Jonathan Edwards, *Representative Selections*, ed. Clarence H. Faust and Thomas H. Johnson, American Century Series (New York: Hill & Wang, 1962), pp. 164–68. Christopher Marlowe, *The Tragicall History of D. Faustus*, 1.312. The "saint" was Innocent of Alaska. See further Gerrish, *Grace and Gratitude*; "The Mirror of God's Goodness"; "Jesus, Myth, and History."

Running the Race (23 April 1989)

Origen, quoted from Eusebius in *Historia Ecclesiastica* 6.20 (291). John Calvin, *Institutes of the Christian Religion*, 3.2.4; this passage is taken from the two-volume translation by Henry Beveridge (London: J. Clarke, [1949]); Miguel de Unamuno, *The Agony of Christianity and Essays on Faith*, trans. Anthony Kerrigan, *Selected Works*, vol. 5 (Princeton, N.J.: Princeton University Press, 1974), pp. 10, 175. The aphorism "All must do their own believing," etc., probably goes back to Martin Luther's *Eight Wittenberg Sermons* (1522). These can be found in *Works of Martin Luther: Philadelphia Edition*, 6 vols. (Philadelphia: Muhlenberg Press, 1915–43). C. D. Broad, *Religion, Philosophy and Psychical Research: Selected Essays* (New York: Humanities Press, 1969), pp. 200–201. See further Gerrish, *Saving and Secular Faith*; "Practical Belief."

Justice (6 May 1984)

Herodotus, *History*, 1.32. The phrase "sacrificial tolls" is from Goethe's "Prometheus." John Calvin, *A Reformation Debate: Sadoleto's Letter to the Genevans and Calvin's Reply—John Calvin and Jacopo Sadoleto*, ed. John C. Olin (Grand Rapids, Baker Book House, 1976). The order and the wording have been changed so as not to have to go into the historical background or the debate with Sadoleto. Roy Larson, *Chicago Sun-Times*, 26 March 1983. See further Gerrish, *Saving and Secular Faith*; "Practical Belief."

The Proof of Friendship (5 May 1991)

Author's note: The New Revised Standard Version translates Psalm 25:14 "the friendship of the LORD." But this is misleading: the word used means "intimacy." John Calvin, *Institutes of the Christian Religion* 3.19.5. See also John Calvin's remarks in his commentary on 1 Timothy 2:5. Cicero, *De amicitia*, 69–71. On "no greater love" see also Aristotle, *Nichomachean Ethics*, 1169a, 1158a (Everyman edition, p. 191; cf. 1171a/230). J. B. Phillips, *Your God Is Too Small* (New York: Macmillan Co., 1960). Epictetus, *Discourses* (Loeb edition), 1:395. Stopford A. Brooke, *Life and Letters of Fredk. W. Robertson, M.A.* (London: Smith, Elder, 1868), p. 82. See further Gerrish, *Grace and Gratitude*; "The Mirror of God's Goodness"; "Theology within the Limits of Piety Alone."

VI. COMPANIONS

The Real Treasure of the Church
(25 October 1987, Bond Chapel)

James Fenimore Cooper, *The Pathfinder; The Inland Sea* (New York: The Modern Library/Random House, 1952), esp. p. 408. Martin Luther, *D. Martin Luthers Werke: Kritische Gesamtausgabe*, Weimarer Ausgabe (Weimar, 1883–), 40^1:343, 17^2:200–204. Thomas Aquinas, *Summa theologiae*, IaIIae, q. 113, a. 9. John Calvin, *Institutes of the Christian Religion* 3.11.1, 19.5. See further Gerrish, *Grace and Gratitude*; "The Chief Article—Then and Now," in *Continuing the Reformation*, pp. 17–37; "Doctor Martin Luther: Subjectivity and Doctrine in the Lutheran Reformation," in *Continuing the Reformation*, pp. 38–56; "By Faith Alone: Medium and Message in Luther's Gospel," in *The Old Protestantism and the New*, pp. 69–89.

The Call to Worship (5 March 1989)

Gregory Dix, *The Shape of the Liturgy* (London: Dacre Press, 1960). Walter D. Edmonds, *Drums along the Mohawk* (Boston: Little, Brown, & Co., [1936]), pp. 156–57. For the remarks by the Puritan, see William D. Maxwell, *Concerning Worship* (Oxford: Oxford University Press, 1948), p. 54. Sir Henry [John] Newbolt, *Collected Poems 1897–1907* (London: Thomas Nelson & Sons, [1910]), pp. 128–30. Vilmos Vajta, *Luther on Worship: An Interpretation* [trans. U.S. Leupold] (Philadelphia: Fortress Press, 1958), for Luther's sermon on worship. See further Gerrish, *Grace and Gratitude*.

The Promise of Baptism (June 1960)

This sermon was preached in Christ Church Presbyterian, Chicago. The hymn is "Bread of the World in Mercy Broken," by Reginald Heber (1827). The comparison of forgiveness to washing is from John Calvin's *Catechism*. Augustine, *Confessions*. The Larger Catechism (1647), in *The Constitution of the Presbyterian*

Church (U.S.A.), Part I: Book of Confessions (New York: Office of the General Assembly, 1983), 7.111–7.306. See further Gerrish, *Grace and Gratitude*, chap. 4.

Remembrance of Things Present (12 February 1995)

Augustine, *Homilies on the Gospel of John*, tractate xxvi, sect. 13. For Luther's comments about the sermon, see Martin Luther, *Babylonian Captivity*, in *Luther's Works*, ed. Jaroslav Pelikan and Helmut T. Lehmann, 55 vols. (St. Louis, Mo: Concordia Publishing House; Philadelphia: Fortress Press, 1955–86), 36:56. Robert Wuthnow, *The Restructuring of American Religion: Society and Faith Since World War II* (Princeton: Princeton University Press, 1988), p. 127. For Luther's remarks about the Lord's Supper, see Martin Luther, *Treatise on the New Testament*, in *Luther's Works*, ed. Jaroslav Pelikan and Helmut T. Lehmann, 55 vols. (St. Louis: Concordia Publishing House; Philadelphia: Fortress Press, 1955–86), 35:85. Matthew Henry is the commentator who makes the observation ad loc. about remembering an absent friend. On "superstitious Christianity," see Alexander Maclaren commentary ad loc. Calvin to Bullinger, 25 Feb. 1547, *Ioannis Calvini opera quae supersunt omnia*, ed. Wilhelm Baum, Eduard Cunitz, and Eduard Reuss, 59 vols., *Corpus Reformatorum*, vols. 29–87 (Brunswick: C.A. Schwetschke & Son [M. Bruhn], 1863–1900), 12:481. Thomas Cranmer, *The Remains of Thomas Cranmer*, ed. Henry Jenkyns, 4 vols., Library of English Literature (Oxford: University Press, 1833), 4:85. See further Gerrish, "Eucharist," *Encyclopedia of the Reformation*, ed. Hans J. Hillerbrand, 4 vols. (New York: Oxford University Press, 1996), 2:71–81; *Grace and Gratitude*; "Discerning the Body: Sign and Reality in Luther's Controversy with the Swiss," in *Continuing the Reformation*, pp. 57–75; "Gospel and Eucharist: John Calvin on the Lord's Supper," in *The Old Protestantism and the New*, pp. 106–17; "Sign and Reality: The Lord's Supper in the Reformed Confessions," in *The Old Protestantism and the New*, pp. 118–30.

VII. PILGRIMS

The Immigrants (4 December 1983)

Ernst Troeltsch, *Christian Thought: Its History and Application*, trans. [F.] von Hügel (New York: Meridian Books, 1957), p. 17. The translation of Philippians 3:20 as "We are citizens of Heaven" comes from J. B. Phillips, *Letters to Young Churches* (London: Geoffrey Bles, 1947). The translation of this verse as "We are a colony of heaven" is from James Moffatt, *A New*

Translation of the Bible: Containing the Old and New Testaments (New York: Harper & Brothers, 1935). For the comments of the "anonymous Christian apologist," see *Letter to Diognetus*, Library of Christian Classics (Philadelphia: Westminster Press, 1960), 1:217–18. Mike Royko, *Boss: Richard J. Daley of Chicago*, (New York: E. P. Dutton & Co., 1971), 25.

Strangers on Earth (4 June 1978)

Blaise Pascal, *Pensées*, nos. 72, 206, 347. Will and Ariel Durant, *The Lessons of History* (New York: Simon & Schuster, [1968]), pp. 14–15. Bertrand Russell, "A Free Man's Worship," in *Why I Am Not a Christian: And Other Essays on Religion and Related Subjects*, ed. Paul Edwards (New York: Simon & Schuster, 1957), p. 111. Catechism by John Calvin, *Catechism of the Church of Geneva* (author's translation from the original). See further Gerrish, "The Secret Religion of Germany."

The Simple Truth (12 February 1984)

Paul Emer More characterizes Paul's use of the potter-clay metaphor "one of the most heart-sickening." More's remarks are quoted in *The Interpreter's Bible*, 12 vols. (New York: Abingdon-Cokesbury Press, 1951–57), 5:962. See further Gerrish, *Saving and Secular Faith*; "Friedrich Schleiermacher (1768–1834)," in *Continuing the Reformation*, pp. 147–77; "By Faith Alone."

One Thing Certain (14 March 1982)

Author's Note: In a personal communication to me, Harris disclaimed originality for the view of education expressed in my opening remarks. R[aymond] B. Blakney, *The Way of Life: A New Translation of the Tao Te Ching* (New York: American Library/Mentor Books, 1955), p. 101. For Erasmus on Christ and the gospel, see John C. Olin, ed., *Christian Humanism and the Reformation: Selected Writings of Erasmus with the Life of Erasmus by Beatus Rhenanus*, rev. ed. (New York: Fordham University Press, 1975), p. 106. Kant's admonition can be found in his essay "What Is Enlightenment?" See Lewis White Beck's translation in *Kant on History*, Library of Liberal Arts (Indianapolis: Bobbs-Merrill Co., 1978), p. 3. Martin Luther, *Eight Wittenberg Sermons* (1522), sermon 1 in *Works of Martin Luther: Philadelphia Edition*, 6 vols. (Philadelphia: Muhlenberg Press, 1915–43), 2:391. Sir Arthur Stanley Eddington, *Science and the Unseen World* (New York: Macmillan Co., 1929), pp. 42–43. John Calvin, commentary ad loc. See further Gerrish, *Saving and Secular Faith*; "By Faith Alone."

Dreamers of the Day (3 October 1982)

Blaise Pascal, *Pensées*, no. 210. Alan Wood, *Bertrand Russell: The Passionate Skeptic* (New York: Simon & Schuster, 1958), pp. 236–37. George Bernard Shaw, *Saint Joan: A Chronicle Play in Six Scenes* (New York: Dodd, Mead & Co., 1936), Scene 1. R. N. Bolles, *What Color Is Your Parachute?: A Practical Manual for Job-Hunters & Career Changers* (Berkeley, Calif.: Ten Speed Press, 1982), p. 308.

WORKS BY B. A. GERRISH

Continuing the Reformation: Essays on Modern Religious Thought. Chicago: University of Chicago Press, 1993.

Grace and Gratitude: The Eucharistic Theology of John Calvin. Minneapolis: Fortress Press, 1993.

The Old Protestantism and the New: Essays on the Reformation Heritage. Chicago: University of Chicago Press; Edinburgh: T. & T. Clark, 1982.

A Prince of the Church: Schleiermacher and the Beginnings of Modern Theology. Philadelphia: Fortress Press, London: SCM Press, 1984.

Saving and Secular Faith: An Invitation to Systematic Theology. Minneapolis: Fortress Press, 1999.